About Island Press

Since 1984, the nonprofit organization Island Press has been stimulating, shaping, and communicating ideas that are essential for solving environmental problems worldwide. With more than 1,000 titles in print and some 30 new releases each year, we are the nation's leading publisher on environmental issues. We identify innovative thinkers and emerging trends in the environmental field. We work with world-renowned experts and authors to develop cross-disciplinary solutions to environmental challenges.

Island Press designs and executes educational campaigns, in conjunction with our authors, to communicate their critical messages in print, in person, and online using the latest technologies, innovative programs, and the media. Our goal is to reach targeted audiences—scientists, policy makers, environmental advocates, urban planners, the media, and concerned citizens—with information that can be used to create the framework for long-term ecological health and human well-being.

Island Press gratefully acknowledges major support from The Bobolink Foundation, Caldera Foundation, The Curtis and Edith Munson Foundation, The Forrest C. and Frances H. Lattner Foundation, The JPB Foundation, The Kresge Foundation, The Summit Charitable Foundation, Inc., and many other generous organizations and individuals.

The opinions expressed in this book are those of the author(s) and do not necessarily reflect the views of our supporters.

Designing the Megaregion

Designing the Megaregion

MEETING URBAN CHALLENGES AT A NEW SCALE

Jonathan Barnett

ISLANDPRESS

Washington | Covelo | London

All rights reserved under International and Pan-American Copyright Conventions. No part of this book may be reproduced in any form or by any means without permission in writing from the publisher: Island Press, 2000 M Street, NW, Suite 650, Washington, DC 20036.

ISLAND PRESS is a trademark of the Center for Resource Economics.

Library of Congress Control Number: 2019948296

All Island Press books are printed on environmentally responsible materials.

Manufactured in the United States of America
10 9 8 7 6 5 4 3 2 1

Keywords: climate change, ecoregion, geographic information systems (GIS), inequity, land use planning, landscape scale, natural disasters, natural environment, passenger rail, real estate development, transit, transportation, urban resilience, zoning

Contents

Foreword

During the past few decades, a phenomenon of urbanization has become more widely observed by academics and urban-policy experts. Around the world, big cities and their large urban and suburban regions are growing together with other metropolitan areas, forming massive conglomerations. These megaregions are capturing much of the world population and economic growth.

Meanwhile, megaregions have attracted the attention of planners, designers, and engineers who view this scale as potentially helpful for addressing challenges that go beyond city limits, such as transportation systems and environmental quality.

In *Designing the Megaregion*, esteemed educator and practitioner Jonathan Barnett addresses these two major foci of megaregions but takes on several related topics as well. First, he is more explicit about the need to design megaregions. In this regard, Barnett goes beyond the more common planning and policy approaches. Second, he introduces the potential role of ecoregions. In doing so, he reinforces the interactive natures and potentials of megaregions. Third, he addresses the issues of inequalities within and beyond megaregions and identifies ways to address them. Finally, he takes on how to adapt government structures to megaregions and how local regulations can be regeared to promote sustainability and equality.

The American economist and political scientist Herbert Simon noted, "To design is to devise courses of actions aimed at changing existing situations into preferred ones." Barnett illustrates how megaregion-scale design can help improve human lives for the better. He suggests that such design can occur incrementally. There's much to juggle, so tackling bits while keeping in mind larger systems, processes, and goals is wise. The adjustment to climate change is related to reducing the congestion of roadways and to making communities more inclusive. In all design, Barnett notes, "the variables are interrelated."

Barnett makes a strong case that one should start with preventing people from settling in stupid places. That is, we should not be allowed to live or work or send our children to school in places that endanger our health, safety, or welfare or that of our loved ones. And, by the way, it is even stupider to rebuild and finance living in places of risk after they have been destroyed by natural or human-assisted disasters.

After we have set aside natural areas that contribute to our well-being (and that of other species too), we can design the elements of our settlement. A promise of the megaregional scale is more effective, what Barnett calls "balanced," transportation. In the United States, the transportation system is out of balance with an overdependence on cars and trucks, which results in increasingly congested roadways and contributes to global warming.

In balanced transportation systems, various modes—walking, biking, driving, riding, flying—are connected thoughtfully and more equitably. As Barnett notes, the national highway system in the United States is largely responsible for megaregions. Inadvertently, interstate highways also resulted in left-behind places. Air travel has likewise created "fly-over" regions.

Barnett advocates megaregional design as a strategy to fix inequalities. For instance, balanced transportation systems improve connections between where people live and where they work. This is especially important for the lower-income people. Likewise, the design of communities to reduce threats of natural disasters from flooding, wildfire, and storm surge benefits the poor, the disabled, the elderly, and the young.

The accomplishment of megaregional design requires the adaptation of existing government structures and the renewal of city policies. One way for governments to adapt is to cooperate. Barnett notes several examples in the United States where jurisdictions collaborate across river basins. These agreements have flood-control, drinking water, water-quality, and recreation benefits. And Barnett indicates that transportation planning is already regional. The challenge is to broaden such cooperation beyond water management and highway building.

Furthermore, local regulations should be rewritten to promote sustainability (and beyond to resilience and regeneration) as well as equity. This will be an ambitious yet necessary undertaking in this first urban century. Jonathan Barnett delivers a hopeful message that this is possible. As he illustrates, the design of megaregions requires ecological literacy and a renewed commitment to social equity.

Frederick R. Steiner
Dean and Paley Professor
University of Pennsylvania Stuart Weitzman School of Design

CHAPTER 1:

A New Scale for Urban Challenges

When you drive along the I-95 corridor on the East Coast of the United States, or the I-5 corridor in the Pacific Northwest, along highways in Florida, or to cities around Chicago, you see that the intervals of open country are getting smaller. New clusters of offices and shopping malls, as big as traditional downtowns, or even bigger, have grown up in what used to be suburbs. New housing developments at the urban edge are expanding to meet the advancing suburbs of neighboring cities. These spreading urban areas have now reached a whole new scale, which has been given a new name: *megaregions*. According to the US Census Bureau, the population of the United States will grow to 438 million by 2050, from 327 million in 2018. Much of this growth is predicted to take place in the cities and suburbs that make up the areas identified as megaregions. These urban places are already extensive. According to one measurement, the proportion of the US population living in urban areas is about 63 percent. Another way of looking at the data puts the people living at an urban density today at more than 80 percent.[1] Megaregions will extend urbanization even more.

Megaregions Are Predictions:
We Still Have a Chance to Shape Them

The growth of megaregions is a statistical projection of what is likely to happen by 2050. There is still time to shape what happens. And reshaping current trends is an urgent matter. The spread of cities has reached a point where construction dominates the environment in many places and puts stress on the natural operating systems that are necessary for our existence. As climate changes in response to these pressures, it becomes more and more critical to design urban development within the ability of nature to sustain it. Economic and population growth also create opportunities to repair environmental damage created by earlier development, and redirect investment to bypassed parts of older cities, which are becoming more separate and unequal. There are three primary issues that need to be addressed in growing megaregions:

- managing how new development will fit into its environmental setting while a warming climate is changing what had once seemed a stable landscape
- building a transportation system that can pull together all the components of these large urban regions
- challenging the forces that make megaregions very unequal places

Resolving these three sets of interrelated problems will produce designs for the evolving megaregions that make them more sustainable, functional, and equitable. Implementation is possible incrementally within systems of management that already exist and are within the powers of state and local governments.

Urban regions have been spreading out for a long time. Back in 1961, the geographer Jean Gottmann described the way urban areas in the northeastern United States were growing together into a new kind of regional city and called it *megalopolis*.[2] Gottmann had detected an emerging trend. There are now many parts of the world where multi-city regions are forming at a similar scale. In the United States, population and economic growth are predicted to concentrate in megaregions, such as the Northeast Corridor Gottmann described, which can now be observed as running from Richmond, Virginia, to Portland, Maine. Another such region is developing from Birmingham, Alabama, through Atlanta to Greenville and Spartanburg, South Carolina, and then on to Charlotte, Greensboro, Raleigh, and Durham, North Carolina. Much of the state of Florida has become a continuous urban area, as is the region south from Santa Barbara through Los Angeles and on to San Diego.[3]

Figure 1-1 is a map prepared by the Regional Plan Association predicting the extent of US megaregions in 2050.[4] Another set of population projections for 2040 is mapped by Arthur Nelson and Robert Lang in their book *Megapolitan America.* They describe twenty-three megapolitan areas grouped in ten megapolitan clusters.[5] Some of the clusters have different names from those chosen by the Regional Plan Association or the Georgia Institute of Technology for another well-known map, and there are also conceptual differences about what urbanized regions belong with one another, but the maps are clearly about the same underlying trend.

Mapping commuting patterns is a way of describing employment relationships among urban areas. Figure 1-2 is a map of commuting patterns in the midwestern part of the United States, part of a 2016 study by Garrett G. D. Nelson of Dartmouth and Alisdair Rae of the University of Sheffield.[6] Their commuter maps, which cover the entire United States, show that megaregions are emerging for economic reasons, and not just from population growth.

Figure 1-2 shows commuting patterns in cities radiating out from Chicago. The Regional Plan Association maps these intercity relationships in figure 1-1 as showing a single Great Lakes megaregion. It is also

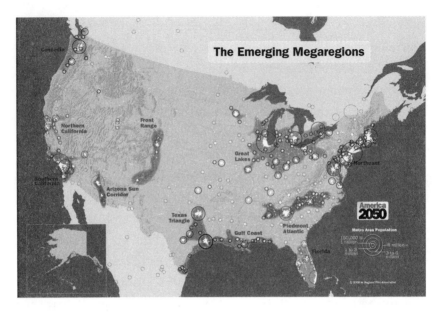

Figure 1-1: Emerging megaregions as mapped by America in 2050, a project of the Regional Plan Association. The regions were identified by population projections to 2050; the initial study was prepared in 2004 at the University of Pennsylvania. The boundaries of megaregions are estimates.

possible to read this diagram as delineating megaregion corridors from Chicago to Saint Louis, Chicago to Detroit, and from Cincinnati to Columbus and on to Cleveland. What is clear is that evolving relationships among cities are creating a new scale of urbanization.

Megaregions have been growing through a process often described as urban sprawl. Why can't these developing areas sit up straight like traditional cities? Why do they keep spreading over the landscape; why are so many older areas left behind? One answer is that current urban growth in the United States is driven by forces deeply embedded in the US economy. There is more money to be made in the land transaction that turns agricultural or woodland acreage into real estate development than in the profit margins for the buildings themselves.

Figure 1-2: One of the maps from "An Economic Geography of the United States: From Commutes to Megaregions," an article published in November 2016 in *PLOS ONE* by Garrett Dash Nelson of Dartmouth College and Alasdair Rae of the University of Sheffield. "We employ a data set of more than 4,000,000 commutes as a proxy for patterns of economic interconnection, given the importance of commutes in structuring the geography of labor markets."

Over the years, real estate companies have grown up that specialize in converting undeveloped land into building lots and houses, often hundreds or even thousands at a time. Turning vacant or lightly used land along a highway, and especially at a highway interchange, into stores, offices, or hotels can also be highly profitable, the work of other kinds of specialized real estate companies. The highways that create prime development sites are paid for by governments, not developers. The market for new houses has been supported by tax deductions for mortgage interest and for property taxes,[7] and by mortgage guarantees from the Federal Housing Administration and from a program that helps veterans buy houses. Two more federal agencies were created to support the secondary market in mortgages, and the Government

National Mortgage Association guarantees mortgage-backed securities. The collapse of mortgage-based securities and the wave of foreclosures beginning in 2008 certainly showed there are limits to the continuing construction of new houses, but housing construction has resumed, and the growth model continues much as it did before the crash.

For families looking for a new home, the fringe of an urban area can offer a bigger house and yard for less money than an older neighborhood closer in, because of government subsidies and the economies of scale that benefit real estate companies when they convert tracts of non-urban land into development. Low taxes on gasoline, compared with taxes in other countries, make trips to and from newly opened locations on the urban fringe more affordable. As people are drawn to new suburban locations, they create new markets for shops and services, which become tenants in new commercial developments. Employers may then relocate to draw on a new labor market, building or becoming tenants in these developing areas. This pattern can repeat over and over, leaving older cities and suburbs with a shrinking economic base where poverty and urban problems are concentrated, motivating more people to seek a better life in a new location.

Regional cities are also growing in other countries, but some of these countries have been able to manage urban growth in ways unavailable in the United States. In Japan the high-speed rail line, the Shinkansen, reinforced by a strong network of local rail services, gives the megaregion that has evolved from Tokyo to Osaka and Kobe a design structure. It supports centers of growth around stations, and a new interrelated economic structure by shortening the time it takes to go between important locations. In the Netherlands the transportation, land preservation, and flood protections for the megaregion that includes Amsterdam, Rotterdam, The Hague, and Utrecht are overseen by the national government. The entire country has a population of about seventeen million, no bigger than some of the megaregions emerging in the United States.

The Need to Design Megaregions

We know how to design downtowns and urban centers. We have good ideas about how to design neighborhoods and suburbs. But planning and urban design have not kept pace with the need to manage growth at the edge of cities, or to restore the economic health of older areas. An important element missing from urban development in the United States is regional design that responds to its environmental context in a constructive way, rather than reengineering nature to conform to standard development patterns. Current development trends are also urbanizing far more land than is necessary to support actual population and economic growth. Rechanneling some of that growth is an opportunity to repair problems in areas that have been bypassed by new investment and correct some of the inequities built into the way cities are growing now. If we had high-speed rail lines, as the nations that are our chief economic competitors now all do, and if we had regional governments at the scale of a small country like the Netherlands, it would be easier to guide the development of the emerging megaregions. But we don't; and it will be many years before we do, if ever.

In 2009, President Barack Obama put forward a plan for high-speed rail lines within many of the developing megaregions in the United States as part of government funding to support economic recovery after the Great Recession. Political opposition stopped progress on all these proposed lines, except for one in California. The central portion of the California line is being constructed, but the important links to San Francisco and to Los Angeles are not yet built, or financed.

Discussions about regional growth management in the United States always refer to the difficulty of coordinating the multiple local governments within each region. Where regional cooperation does take place, it is usually about new highways. When regional development has grown across state lines, cooperation has required regional compacts among states, usually dealing with issues such as allocating the water supply and preserving water quality.

The Minneapolis–Saint Paul Metropolitan Council, which we will come back to in chapter 9, is one of the few successful US prototypes for regional government. Metro, the local government for Greater Portland, Oregon, is another well-known example. But it does not cover the portion of the region that is across the border in the state of Washington and manages only a fraction of the evolving megaregion that extends from Eugene, Oregon, up to Tacoma and Seattle, and then up to the Canadian border and on to Vancouver, British Columbia.

Even when a megaregion is all within one state, state governments generally let smaller local governments make decisions about land use and growth management. The Los Angeles–San Diego region continues to have many local governments within it, plus Tijuana, Mexico, which is contiguous to San Diego and has some close economic ties to it, but is, of course, in another country.

Waiting for high-speed rail and new forms of regional government to create a sustainable development strategy for megaregions could take a very long time, while current growth pressures continue, and the path to achieving regional design becomes more difficult.

Designing Regions Incrementally

Megaregions may not look like design problems, but guiding their growth demands the same kind of thinking that goes into urban design decisions at smaller scales. There are many variables to consider and many alternative arrangements about how to relate the built environment to nature, and to existing urban development; about how to preserve what is good about an area and repair what can be improved; about how to organize streets, infrastructure, and the different modes of transportation; about how to make places that are attractive to everyone, and how to correct the inequalities that are built into current urban development.

To start reshaping megaregions to safeguard the natural environment and adapt to climate change, to reduce congestion on highways and at airports, and to open up communities to be more equitable and inclusive, we need to design sustainable regional growth incrementally, without having to wait for major national policy changes or whole new governmental structures.

Relating development to the natural environment has become more feasible because geographic information systems (GIS) are now available to states and almost all local governments. GIS can make accurate information about land contours, streams, and soil conditions for a whole community available to decision-makers, who have had to depend before on the limited information available from surveys of individual properties. The availability of detailed environmental information makes it possible to establish a context for regional design: showing what natural systems need to be preserved from the destabilizing effects of development and also showing where the natural environment is changing in response to a warming climate.

Another major missing piece in achieving a design for growing megaregions has been train service, not necessarily as fast as high-speed trains in Europe and Asia, but fast enough to draw passengers from short trips on airplanes and from driving—reducing congestion on highways and at airports. The success of the Acela Express intercity train service in the Northeast has caused private investors to become interested in providing faster passenger train service in other megaregions, including Florida, Texas, and the route from Los Angeles to Las Vegas. It has also encouraged states to start planning with Amtrak for upgraded passenger rail service in other megaregions. Train service by itself is not enough to balance transportation in a megaregion, but innovations in bus rapid transit, and improved street designs with landscaped sidewalks and protected bicycle lanes, can reduce reliance on cars and make more places walkable and accessible by bicycle.

The abandonment of substantial areas in older cities has now reached a point where it has become an opportunity as well as a tragedy. There is so much land available that it is possible to imagine transformative investments taking place in the inner city. The vacant stores along commercial corridors in the suburbs, a consequence of e-commerce and other changes in retail shopping, are another opportunity, as these commercial corridors are fast becoming land banks. Rezoning land in these corridors for town houses and apartments will be an opportunity to offer more affordable housing in suburbs and, with subsidies, more housing choices for people who cannot afford market-rate rentals.

As in all design processes, the variables are interrelated. Balancing transportation within megaregions is a way to make more jobs available to people living where there has been little transit access, and it is also a way of channeling development away from environmentally sensitive parts of the landscape. Addressing the inequalities that are built into megaregions—and have been a significant factor in the way megaregions are growing—can take development pressures off the urban fringe and make trains and transits more effective. While reducing spatial inequalities will not eliminate other aspects of unfairness in our society, it can help make affordable housing closer to where people who need it want to live and work.

Designing megaregions can begin right now, using government institutions that already exist and development concepts that will work in today's real estate market. Design can begin in parts of the megaregion, and successes in one place can inspire emulation. Landscape Conservation Cooperatives; multistate compacts for managing flooding, water supplies, and rail transportation; coastal zone management commissions; state planning and environmental agencies; the metropolitan planning organizations that exist in every state; local administration of water and sewer districts, and of zoning and subdivision code—all these governmental mechanisms exist now and can be enlisted in design processes for megaregions.

These regional and local agencies have different boundaries, and different ways of operating. Over time, it may be that several of them should be consolidated. Possibly a regional form of governance will grow up to manage the evolving megaregions, but in the meantime, regional design can be implemented through a network of existing institutions.

There is an urgent need to begin designing megaregions, and the ways to make it happen are already available.

CHAPTER 2:

Recognizing Ecoregions as the Context for Development

The United States Environmental Protection Agency (EPA) defines *ecoregions* as geographical areas where "the type, quality, and quantity of the environmental resources . . . are generally similar."[1] The many different ecoregions within the United States span across state borders and rarely fit within the boundaries of the governments that are building highways and airports or approving new development.

The EPA maps the ecoregions of the United States at four levels of similarity from twelve large regions down to much smaller local areas:

At the largest scale, Level I, the whole eastern part of the United States is seen as one region except for the tip of Florida and woodlands in northern New England; the Great Plains are mapped as one region as well.

At Level II, islands at the tip of Florida, plus the Everglades, Miami, and Miami Beach, are located within the Southern Florida Coastal Plain, described as a tropical wet forest. Most of the rest of Florida is in the Southeast Coastal Plain, an area of high water tables that extends northward into Georgia. Much of northern New England and the western parts of Massachusetts and Connecticut are in the Atlantic Highlands

Level II ecoregion, a forested area with poor soils and many glacial lakes.

Each of the 104 Level III ecoregions mapped in the United States has its own distinctive climate, vegetation, and soil conditions. Within each of these ecoregions there are further distinctive Level IV subdivisions. Figure 2-1 is a map of what the EPA designates as Level III and IV ecoregions in the state of Washington. Their complex boundaries have no relation to political jurisdictions.

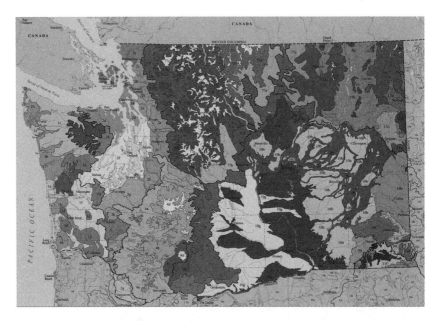

Figure 2-1: This map of Washington State's Level III and IV ecoregions, prepared by the United States Environmental Protection Agency, shows the boundaries of major ecological areas, which have little relation to political jurisdictions. Rapidly urbanizing land increases the conflicts between development and what is needed to maintain and enhance natural systems.

As urban development expands at the scale of the megaregion, it takes over more and more of the surrounding natural environment, altering it permanently and tipping the ecological balance in many places. More frequent and widespread flooding in the last few decades is partly a result of increased rainfall from a warming climate, but another significant cause is the amount of natural landscape being reshaped by bulldozers and paved as streets and parking lots. Development is also moving more and more people into places where they are at risk from floods, wildfires, and other natural hazards.

Heat waves also become more intense as more of the landscape is covered by heat-absorbing pavement and rooftops. Droughts become more of a problem as roofs and paving cause rainwater to run off quickly into streams and rivers, instead of being absorbed into the natural landscape to refill the aquifers that are the water supply in many regions. A continually warming climate is likely to turn today's serious problems into frequently recurring disasters if there are no plans to prevent them. Preserving development from environmental catastrophes should have a political constituency including both builders and buyers.

The Urgent Need to Relate Development to the Natural Landscape

Governmental assessments of the impact of a development on the natural environment have been confined to the consideration of individual projects—with the review usually done by towns and cities, and sometimes by counties. So far, attempts to design development within the context of natural systems have failed, or have been effective for only small aspects of the much larger problem. Excluding areas from development that are known to be subject to flooding, not building on hillsides with steep slopes, being careful in developing land with soil conditions subject to erosion are all necessary steps in developing a regional design. Coastal zones, natural habitats, recharge areas for aquifers, and prime agricultural land should also be subject to development restrictions so that they can be part of an overall ecodesign concept for regional development.

The restoration of important natural systems within existing urban areas is an equally important aspect of regional ecodesign. Parks and reservations of land preserved in a natural state can become the components of a larger, connected open-space system. Streams that have been channeled or put in culverts can be opened up and restored. New landscapes can be created in bypassed and brownfield areas by building landscape frameworks that allow natural systems to take over. And the overall scenic appearance of a region can be carefully curated and cultivated, to the benefit of everyone.

Right now, the mechanisms for managing growth in such desirable directions mostly exist at the local level, but there are regional planning agencies and interstate compacts that could assume a stronger role in helping local governments manage and coordinate growth, using new computer-based technologies that can be shared among communities within a megaregion. How to use these new technologies is discussed in the next chapter.

A Changing Climate Makes Environmental Preservation Even More Important

A changing climate has made the relationship between an urbanizing region and its natural setting an even more critical issue. Greenhouse gases already in the atmosphere make substantial changes in the climate inevitable by 2050, regardless of any potential success in mitigating the causes of climate change. Designing and planning for growth by 2050 must consider the ways global warming will alter the ability of the natural environment to accept urban and suburban development.

Coastal storm surges, river floods, and local flash floods are all becoming more severe problems. Summers are becoming hotter and periods of drought longer. Wildfires are affecting more people almost every year. Should development continue in vulnerable areas? What should be done to safeguard existing development? Are there areas that should be returned to a natural state? These questions need to be answered with regard to both coastal cities and the communities that have grown up in forested areas. Communities along rivers face similar issues.

In 2013 the Rockefeller Foundation funded a program, 100 Resilient Cities, to help representative cities around the world develop a shared methodology for managing a broad range of physical, social, and economic challenges, including the stresses created in urban areas by a warming climate. Each city has been encouraged to develop a resilience strategy, drawing on experts but discussing all aspects of the strategy in public forums. The Rockefeller Foundation is phasing out its funding for 100 Resilient Cities, but the influence of the program remains significant.

Coastal Floods: Norfolk, Virginia, was selected as a Resilient City, and one of its major challenges is regular tidal flooding of streets and houses in neighborhoods that never used to flood, a forerunner of much worse flooding problems as sea levels rise and storm events become more severe and more frequent. Figure 2-2 is an aerial view of waterfront neighborhoods in Norfolk, Virginia. Norfolk went through a planning process called Norfolk 2100 as part of its resilience strategy, which included mapping the projected one-hundred-year floodplain once sea level in the Norfolk area has risen by three feet. What no one knows for sure is when a three-foot rise will have taken place. Figure 2-3 shows that much of the Hampton Roads area is at risk from flood tides as sea levels rise, and especially from the way that rising seas will amplify storm surges the next time the Hampton Roads area is hit by a hurricane.

Only a few years ago, the Intergovernmental Panel on Climate Change was projecting that a meter of sea level rise (a little more than three feet) was at the upper end of what was likely by 2100. Now some studies suggest that, taking account of melting Arctic and Antarctic ice, there could be three feet of sea level rise by 2050. Recent hurricanes

Figure 2-2: This aerial view of the East Beach neighborhood in Norfolk, Virginia, shows the close relationship between the layout of the city and its waterways. Little Creek, in the center of the photo, is a good location for marinas, which, along with proximity to the beach, have helped attract people to living in Norfolk. In the foreground is one of Norfolk's many US Navy installations. Today, rising sea levels have caused tidal flooding of houses and streets to happen regularly, in clear weather. Almost the whole city is in one of the state of Virginia's four hurricane evacuation zones.

and storms have shown what can happen today to places like New York City and the Houston Ship Channel as storm surges cause extensive damage. Destruction will become even worse as sea levels rise, as higher seas amplify the height and extent of storm surge. While tidal flooding can be managed with seawalls—assuming there is no saltwater intrusion through the ground under the walls—preparing for storm surges in the next thirty years will take major efforts. The initial coastal defenses in the Netherlands, begun after a devastating storm in 1953, took about thirty years to implement.

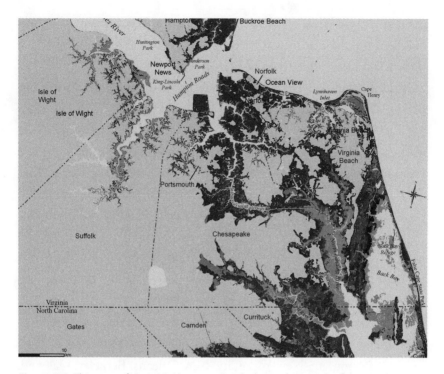

Figure 2-3: This map of Virginia's Hampton Roads shows that much of the area is vulnerable to rising sea levels. Norfolk, in the center of the map, was selected by the Rockefeller Foundation to be one of 100 Resilient Cities worldwide, and the foundation helped fund a study, Vision 2100, to consider the future of Norfolk in a changing climate. The Vision 2100 strategy is to protect Naval Station Norfolk and the city's downtown by whatever structural means are necessary, direct new development to the higher ground at the center of the city, and—over time—make the necessary adaptations to areas at most risk of flooding, which could include raising structures and even phasing out residential development.

Norfolk's strategy is to use engineering to defend the city's two main economic generators: Naval Station Norfolk and Downtown Norfolk, along the Elizabeth River. Available engineering measures include using floodwalls and raising land, streets, and buildings. There is higher ground in the center of Norfolk, and the city's policy will be to increase the density and make it easier to develop there. Some of the neighborhoods in the floodplain will need to have houses and streets raised, or their occupancy will need to be phased out.

Boston is another city that, through its Climate Ready Boston initiative, is taking action to deal with projected flooding. The city compiled predictions about sea level rise and the probabilities of increased frequency and intensity of storm events, and then identified exposed locations. Each vulnerable place then becomes the subject of a planning study with extensive participation from the adjacent communities, developing specific protection measures and adding them to the city's capital improvement program. An important principle in Boston has been to use the funds necessary for protection to create amenities for each community. For example, seawalls are planned as landscaped berms that are incorporated into parkland.

Other Rockefeller Resilient Cities in the United States that have identified hurricanes and coastal flooding as major problems, besides Norfolk and Boston, are New York City, New Orleans, Berkeley, Oakland, Honolulu, Houston, and Greater Miami-Dade County, which includes the cities of Miami and Miami Beach. The website for 100 Resilient Cities says that projected maximum sea level rises would inundate large sections of Miami-Dade County. This is a region where hurricanes are highly probable, with almost two million people living within projected storm surge areas, many without the resources to recover from the loss of property and income that a hurricane can bring.[2]

The problems of the selected 100 Resilient Cities are examples of challenges that extend not only to other coastal cities but along the entire Eastern Seaboard, as well as the Gulf Coast. Not just the cities are at risk, but any development close to the shore is vulnerable, including highways and railway lines. The future of the Northeast, Florida, and Texas megaregions will need to fit into limits established by ocean flooding. Other coastal development will also face comparable restrictions.

On the West Coast, the flat land around the edges of San Francisco Bay is especially at risk from sea level rise.

River Floods: Recent record flooding along rivers in the Midwest of the United States has shown that the network of levees protecting farms and cities—which may have been adequate when they were built—are becoming ineffective as volumes of water increase because of a changing climate. Two thousand nineteen saw major levee breaches along the Missouri, Arkansas, and Mississippi Rivers.[3] The American Society of Civil Engineers (ASCE), in its 2017 Infrastructure Report Card, estimates that $80 billion in construction funds will be needed to maintain and improve US levees to the extent required by 2030. All the levees need to be inspected and evaluated.

The ASCE recommends funding the National Levee Safety Program passed by Congress as part of the Water Resources Reform and Development Act of 2014, which has never been given its necessary appropriations. The report recommends assessing the thirty thousand miles of levees in the United States "using updated hydrology and hydraulic analyses that incorporate the impact of urbanization and climate change, particularly for coastal levees." It may be that in some places traditional engineering will need to be supplemented by "greener" measures, such as making more space for floodwaters by moving the levees back, requiring changes to traditional farm and settlement patterns. Every US megaregion will be confronted with finding improved ways to manage river floods.

Flash Floods: Climate change is demonstrating that many areas of the suburban United States have been developed to the point where stormwater is running off too quickly. Suburban areas that are not near a coast or river can suddenly find streets flooding and basements—and sometimes ground floors—filling up with water. Wells in the same communities can be running dry, as the stormwater quickly drains away without recharging the ground water. These problems can be ameliorated by means of changes in development regulations and retro-fitting existing properties, but such measures will require an extensive, regionally coordinated effort.

Wildfire: As the climate warms, and longer, warmer growing seasons in the United States move northward, forests become less adapted to their current geographic location. Longer warm seasons favor insects that feed on trees. Droughts are also becoming longer and more frequent. Trees are weakened and begin to die, so they become more susceptible to fire.

Unlike rising sea levels, this situation is self-limiting. Wildfires are a natural process; eventually growth will return, favoring species better adapted to new conditions. But the transition period will be very difficult for development close to or within forested areas, and will require rethinking current definitions and policies for the wildland–urban interface (WUI), along with improved forest maintenance. The 2017 Tubbs Fire in California engulfed the Coffey Park neighborhood of Santa Rosa, which was outside the WUI, indicating that the distances thought to be protective from a spreading fire are not sufficient.

In 2018, the entire community of Paradise, California, was destroyed in the Camp Fire. Paradise was within the WUI. Were there any fire-protection measures, such as vegetation-free surrounding belts and fireproof construction—which could be mandated by building and zoning codes (and are generally not today)—that could have saved this community, or is the continued existence of such communities too dangerous to continue? What other protective measures could be effective? Should there be much more stringent regulations of power lines, given that a defective power line was the probable cause of the Camp Fire? Would better forest management, such as the clearing of the flammable understory, reduce fire hazards?

Figure 2-4 is a map developed by the SILVIS Lab at the University of Wisconsin–Madison that highlights areas of development that are on the edge of forests or mixed into forested areas, not just in California but across the United States. The eastern half of the country could actually be more at risk than California as warming seasons begin to cause

Figure 2-4: This map prepared by the SILVIS Lab at the University of Wisconsin–Madison contains an alarming message. The dark dots on the map are areas that are at the interface between wildlands and urban areas, or are places where buildings and wildland are intermixed. On the left of the map, in California, you can see the dots that represent at-risk areas. Despite the recent news stories about terrible wildfires in California, the number of places at risk is relatively small.

By contrast, the eastern part of the United States and areas of Texas and Minnesota show many of the dark dots. Early settlements took place by clearing the forest, and the forest has come back in some places and is intertwined with development. The same forces that have increased fire risk in the West are starting to take hold in the East: changes in growing seasons that make trees less well-adapted to their locations, increasing insect infestations that weaken trees, with higher average temperatures in the summer. Fortunately, the East is much less susceptible to drought. However, a third of all houses in the United States are in the wildland–urban interface or the intermix; most of those houses are in places where people have not thought there was any fire danger at all.

die-offs of trees. In the United States, approximately one in three houses and one in ten hectares would be at risk of burning if the neighboring woods catch fire.[4]

Drought: Drought is a major issue already in the western United States. Drought conditions will become more frequent and last longer, according to estimates of the future climate. Aside from increasing the risk of wildfire, drought puts stress on farms, which have to rely more on irrigation, and cities run the risk of running out of potable water. Places at risk from drought need better policies for agriculture, including the kinds of crops planted and the way irrigation is managed. Urban areas need to make much more use of recycled water, and places that have access to seawater may have to rely partly on desalination plants—which create serious environmental problems that need to be solved.

Las Vegas, Nevada, relies on Lake Mead, created by the Hoover Dam, for its water. There are competing needs for water from this reservoir, rainfall is diminishing, and the water levels are going down quickly. The situation is not likely to go back to levels established in earlier days, and may become worse. There is a possibility that Las Vegas could run out of water—as Capetown, South Africa, almost did in 2018. Capetown is building desalination plants, but this option is not available for inland Las Vegas, which will have to rely on conservation and recycling even after moving its intake pipe close to the bottom of the lake. What is the likely water budget for Las Vegas in 2030? What measures will Las Vegas need to implement to be able to stay within this allotment? Will successful implementation require re-piping hotels and other buildings to reuse gray water for flushing toilets? What happens to swimming pools and golf courses? What ordinances will be needed to enforce what is necessary? Can Las Vegas also supply some of its water needs from recycled water by having the sewage treatment plants provide drinkable water, as is done in Singapore with what they call NEWater? Water management is always a regional issue. What will need to be done to implement measures necessary by 2030; by 2050?

Heat Waves: A changing climate also means more and longer heat waves. One way to define a heat wave is a period of five or more days when the temperature rises above 95 degrees Fahrenheit, 35 degrees Celsius. The maximum temperature during periods of high heat is going to go up. How much hotter will it get, and where will these heat waves be most intense? Energy consumption will need to increase in order to maintain the necessary indoor temperatures. Will there be days when it will not be safe for some people to go outdoors; will there be midday periods when no one should go outdoors?

There are ways to reduce heat in urban areas, including extensive tree planting, green parking lots, shade structures in public places, and reflective rooftops. But there is only so much such improvements can accomplish. Phoenix, Arizona, already can have three or four weeks at a time with temperatures over 100 degrees Fahrenheit, according to a 2019 article in *Sierra*, the magazine of the Sierra Club, which asked the question: "Can Phoenix Remain Habitable?"[5]

Food Shortages: The world's population is increasing at the same time a changing climate is making it harder to grow food in many places. While the United States is fortunate in having a large agricultural land supply, demand for food is going to increase, both because of more people living in the United States and because of shortages worldwide. At the same time, changing growing seasons will shift the optimal locations for many crops. River flooding may make fertile bottomlands, currently used for agriculture, less available in the future. Water shortages may make certain crops—almonds, for example—less feasible. The United States is currently dependent on a complex international food-supply network, which may be disrupted by climate change. What can be done to preserve the current abundant food culture and continue exports to less-fortunate countries?

Many smaller countries, such as Korea and the Netherlands, grow a substantial quantity of their food in greenhouses. The greenhouse is a way of controlling growing-season temperatures and making relatively small land areas more productive. They are also a way to create food that is locally grown and not subject to the decline in food quality that is the result of the industrialization of agriculture. Greenhouses can be erected over soil, but an especially interesting alternative is building greenhouses on rooftops in urban areas. Large buildings with a regular column structure, such as warehouses, factories, big-box retail, and parking garages, have the potential to be retrofitted to support greenhouses at their roof levels. Prototypes already exist in Brooklyn and Montreal, for example. How would the widespread use of urban greenhouses affect the quantity and quality of the US food supply? What would be needed to scale up a few special examples into general use?

What will the agricultural map of the United States look like in 2050? Which currently productive areas are likely to be less productive because of the changing climate? What needs to be done to conserve or restore soils or both? Especially important: Which areas need to be protected from urbanization in order to ensure the food supply?

For many years, people were able to assume that the natural environment was both stable and indestructible, no matter how natural resources were exploited. Both these assumptions have turned out to be false. The number of people in the world, and the land they have altered and urbanized, has helped to change the climate, and the changing climate in turn is changing the natural landscape. The increasing risks from a warming climate have become enforcement mechanisms for environmental preservation. What may once have seemed to be a matter of choice is now becoming a matter of survival.

CHAPTER 3:

Relating Development to the Natural Environment

Twenty-two Landscape Conservation Cooperatives (LCCs) were established in 2010 across the United States, funded and coordinated by the Fish and Wildlife Service of the US Department of the Interior. Each of these conservation districts represents a relatively self-contained and consistent landscape, but unlike the EPA ecoregions, an LCC takes state boundaries into account. Each cooperative has a staff coordinator, a science coordinator, and a steering committee made up of representatives from different levels of government and also from nongovernmental organizations. Landscape-conservation designs, created by these cooperatives through an open process involving the relevant stakeholders, use computer models to combine information about the physical landscape and its living inhabitants and then highlight the critical places for protecting species, habitats, and the natural landscape across an entire region. By coordinating the latest research and geographic information system (GIS) mapping, these cooperatives have been identifying the parts of the landscape that should have the highest conservation priority and creating databases that can be drawn upon by state and local governments to implement specific policies, such as determining zoning districts.

Figure 3-1 is a GIS map of land-conservation priorities compiled by pulling together research from several LCCs, including the South Atlantic, Peninsular Florida, Gulf Coast Plains and Ozarks, and Gulf Coast Prairie cooperatives. The darkest areas have the highest conservation priority. The South Atlantic LCC has also elected to include conservation issues for its offshore areas.

Figure 3-2 is a computer-generated map of probable urban development for the same region. The darkest areas are those already urbanized.

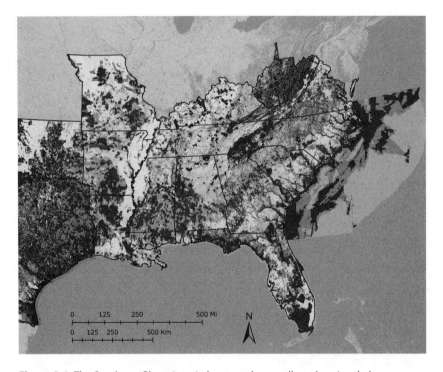

Figure 3-1: The Southeast Blueprint stitches together smaller subregional plans prepared by individual LCCs into a map of conservation and restoration values across the Southeast. The darkest areas have the highest conservation priority. The South Atlantic cooperative has also included offshore conservation issues. This GIS map is remade every year to incorporate the latest improvements to the maps prepared by the subregional cooperatives.

The map clearly shows three megaregions as they are predicted to have developed by mid-century: the South Atlantic megaregion at right, the Florida megaregion below, and at left, the Texas megaregion, sometimes called the Texas Triangle.

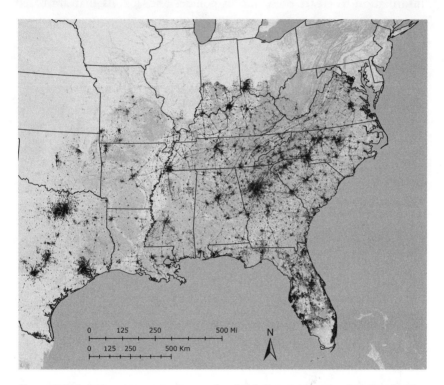

Figure 3-2: A computer-generated map of probable future urban development for the same region can be compared with the previous map. The development map clearly shows emerging megaregions as they are predicted to have developed by mid-century. This analysis makes it possible to prepare a long-range conservation plan to preserve areas that would otherwise be threatened by development.

It is also possible to break down predicted development by decade, to see which priority areas are likely to be under immediate development pressure, followed by measures to conserve threatened areas. This conservation versus development analysis must be repeated regularly, as diverting development from one area can increase pressures on others.

As these maps are based on detailed information and recorded in GIS, it is possible to compare them in relatively fine-grained detail and determine which priority conservation areas are most likely to be threatened by development. State and local governments can use this information to create preservation policies and actions that are based on well-documented, objective information that had not been available previously except for individual properties.

Although there is money in the federal budget to support LCCs, the Trump administration is reported to have choked off their funding.[1] Trying to stop this kind of research is shortsighted. Conservation is about not just preserving the natural landscape but also saving the built environment from natural disasters, as discussed in the previous chapter.

Designing with Nature in a Changing Climate

Each local environment has evolved over time in response to natural forces. Vegetation adapts to the climate; the roots of grasses, trees, and plants stop land eroding from wind and rain; the living creatures become the ones best suited to living in each environment. Ian McHarg in *Design with Nature*, an influential book first published in 1969, made a convincing case that buildings, streets, and landscape should be designed in harmony with their natural context, rather than subduing nature by clearing all trees and bushes, bulldozing land into new shapes, and rechanneling water into culverts and drainpipes.[2] These common practices can destabilize an entire landscape, McHarg warned, leading to flooding, erosion, and more exposure to extreme weather events.

When McHarg wrote his book, nature was still evolving so slowly that it could be considered the same from year to year. Today a changing climate has made the future of each regional landscape much less predictable. Coastal storm surges, flooding along rivers, and flash floods from local downpours occur every few years at an intensity that used to be expected only once in a century. Protracted droughts, heat waves, and damaging forest fires are also happening more often. Some of these natural disasters are the result of exactly the development practices that McHarg warned against. Others are caused by an increasing world population dependent on burning modern fossil fuels, which make oceans and air temperatures warmer, and alter the way wind and water currents flow around the globe.

There is now a need to pay even more attention to natural forces when designing new development, which means understanding nature as a system in which everything is connected. A change in the amount of water that flows out of one property can increase flooding in other places farther downstream. Clearing land for development can cause soils to erode. Warmer summers increase the amount of time that insects can feed on tree leaves, causing die-offs of trees, which can lead to forest fires, endangering homes and other buildings that used to be able to coexist with nearby woodlands. Barry Commoner's 1971 book, *The Closing Circle*, was a comprehensive warning about the conflict between modern industrial society and natural forces.[3] Commoner put forward laws of ecology. Among Commoner's laws are the following:

Everything is connected to everything else.

Everything must go somewhere.

Nature knows best.

There is no such thing as a free lunch. (Every gain is won at some cost.)

Unlike Ian McHarg, Commoner refrained from putting forward solutions, instead saying that dealing with such problems could mean "changing the course of history."

A changing environment can be addressed locally and incrementally, and McHarg showed a way to do this by identifying the natural areas critical to the safety of local communities using objective criteria. McHarg promoted a method of mapping land in terms of its sensitivity to being destabilized by building construction. In his day, it was a laborious process of recording different environmental characteristics by hand on sheets of transparent paper. Today these maps are made on computers using programs partly inspired by McHarg's methods, with information recorded in layers.

The problem for all local governments has been what to do about the kind of information McHarg produced from government survey maps, which were only accurate enough to make decisions about policy, not construction. If a planning commission wanted accurate environmental information for a specific property, it had to be requested from the developer of the project before them, who would commission a survey—covering only the developer's property—so only a small fraction of the local natural systems could be considered.

Another fundamental problem for most planning commissions has been the zoning ordinances they were administering, which had defined the allowable development for each piece of property without any regard for the factors that McHarg mapped. Steep slopes, floodplains, even parts of a property that were always underwater, had each been given the same allowable amount of development as the level upland meadows that McHarg found to be the best place for new construction.

The McHargian method of excluding environmentally sensitive land from development is counter to property rights established by zoning. At first it looked as if the answer to this problem was to make a deal with each developer to transfer the development rights from, for example, a steep hillside to the more level parts of the property, rather than bulldozing the hillside into flat sites, which was the usual way of realizing the zoning potential. This well-known alternative zoning, called planned unit development (PUD) or cluster zoning, has had some success in preserving parts of the natural landscape, but it is always fragmentary, and many developers prefer to exercise their property rights in the usual way, and not engage in negotiations with planning authorities over an alternative site plan.

In 1980, Lane Kendig proposed that parts of a property that were not appropriate for development should not be counted fully when computing the site area in an application for zoning approval. The site area is the basis for determining the amount of square feet of building that can be permitted, so discounting the site area reduces the amount of permitted development. Kendig proposed a 100 percent discount for bluffs, beaches, floodplains, erosion-hazard areas, and underwater land. Steep slopes would be discounted based on the degree of slope. If the slope was greater than 60 degrees, only 5 percent of the land could be counted toward zoning calculations—down to slopes of 15 degrees, where 60 percent of the land could be included in the calculation. Certain types of soils and prime agricultural land were also discounted.[4] Because the whole site remains zoned in the conventional way, Kendig's alternative still requires using PUD to transfer construction to the buildable parts of a site, although it does reduce the allowable amount the zoning permits.

The real question, considered too political to be answered by McHarg or Kendig, is why land that is manifestly unsuitable for development should have any zoning entitlement at all. And why should land suitable for only light development be zoned for anything more intense?

As we can see in figure 3-1, GIS technology has now made it possible to understand the kinds of issues McHarg identified at the scale of the city, region, and megaregion. Understanding at this scale is a critical first step in designing development that is compatible with its natural surroundings.

Local governments now have the detailed information necessary to make objective determinations about the carrying capacity of individual properties based on an understanding of their position in the larger ecological region. Computer-based GIS and high-resolution, lidar-based maps can provide enough detail to make decisions about what land is most suitable for development, and to reduce what is permissible for land that is less suitable.[5] In order for such determinations to be sustainable legally, they need to be incorporated in environmental management plans that can be adopted by local governments and become the basis for converting the existing zoning to a code that takes environmental factors into account.

An Environmentally Based Zoning Ordinance

Urbanizing agricultural, woodland, and beachfront areas is highly profitable, and the profits are boosted by government subsidies for highway construction and home-buying. However, the amount of land that continues to be urbanized is much larger than is needed to accommodate population growth, with new construction drawing people and jobs from older areas. Local governments cannot manage regional development trends independently. Protecting the landscape at the edges of urbanized areas needs to be associated with designing transportation systems to create incentives for development in locations that are environmentally suitable, or have previously been passed over for new investment. Another important initiative: opening up older suburbs to town houses and apartments, which can draw people away from the urban fringe where much of this type of housing is currently being built. These policies are described later in this book.

Local governments are on the front line in managing urban growth, and development regulation is one of their principal management tools, along with street mapping and funding new infrastructure. It is up to the states to make sure local governments have the authority to write the rules to protect the environment, now that there are tools to do this. Some states may need to amend their enabling legislation for local zoning; in other states, local governments may already have the powers they need.

Watersheds as Environmental Zones

States and local governments can also use watersheds as an important legal context for rewriting development regulations to include environmental factors. The watershed can be considered the equivalent of a design that needs to be preserved, in the same sense that a district of historic buildings forms an urban context that should be preserved. An architect resolves an intricate set of interrelated concerns about structure, weather resistance, heat, light, and the activities of the people who will occupy the building being designed. The evolution of a landscape also resolves a complex set of interrelated variables: Water draining into streams and rivers shapes the hills and valleys that form a region's geography, the end product of complicated forces such as the underlying geology and soil, streams and bodies of water, the effects of rain and floods on the drainage system, the weather, and the consequences of all such factors on the plants and animals native to each region, including beavers and humans.

Most of the environmentally sensitive areas identified by Ian McHarg are parts of watersheds. Although everything in nature is connected, watersheds—the areas drained by rivers and their tributaries—create a series of distinctive places, each with its own natural boundary. Watersheds, and their sub-watersheds around tributary streams, are separated from one another by a ridgeline. The suitability of land for development depends on its position within a watershed. Regulatory districts based on watersheds at a variety of scales could become fundamental ways of relating regional development to the natural environment.

However, land has often been developed in opposition to a watershed's natural boundaries. Early settlers regularly built their communities along the local ridgelines, knowing that would keep them safest from flooding, and political boundaries frequently were drawn along river valleys. And, of course, the rectangular geometry used by surveyors has dominated the drawing of jurisdictional boundaries, just as it has defined property lines. The result is that most communities are in more than one local watershed, and property lines and boundaries do not relate to natural contours and drainage patterns.

Even when cities, towns, and counties eventually adopt environmentally based zoning districts, their administration within a watershed is still likely to be fragmentary. There can be several local governments within even a small river watershed, and many local governments include parts of more than one watershed. However, there are already regional governmental structures that are administering watersheds. Making use of these structures to coordinate local regulations is discussed in chapter 9.

Urban Growth Boundaries

States have another means of protecting natural areas from development. In 1973 the Oregon state legislature passed a law requiring cities to map a boundary at their perimeter beyond which no urban development will be permitted. This is an old idea, going back at least to an 1898 book by Ebenezer Howard, who advocated mapping a greenbelt of agricultural land around cities in order to permanently contain urban expansion. Howard proposed that new growth should take place beyond the greenbelt in satellite towns that combined the advantages of living in an urban area with being close to the countryside. Each of these towns would be limited in size and would also have a greenbelt.[6] This idea and related concepts of new towns and garden cities have influenced planning and urban design all over the world.[7]

In Oregon the growth boundary was intended to protect highly productive agricultural land from development, but it was also about efficient use of public money by not extending utilities and other urban services until their construction is fully justified. The law requires each jurisdiction that meets the requirements of the act to provide an estimated twenty years of buildable land within its growth boundary, and the boundary must be reviewed and extended periodically to maintain the budget of land for future development. The growth boundary is really about land as a commodity, not an ecosystem. The law requires communities to expand first into areas not suitable for farming, but there is still local discretion in deciding where the boundary should be extended.

The Portland metropolitan area now has close to fifty years of experience operating within a growth boundary, and results are clearly visible and often studied. There are places around the periphery where intense suburban development stops right at the legal limit, with farmland extending beyond. And within the urban area, there are far fewer abandoned or skipped-over properties than are seen in most places, and development is taking place at higher densities. The growth boundary is not the only factor making Greater Portland unusually cohesive and filled with compactly developed neighborhoods. The Metro government is an important reason, as are the efficient local trolley and light-rail systems.

The frequently made argument against Portland's growth boundary is that it has driven up the price of housing, making it far less affordable than—a frequent comparison—Houston. The argument runs that, if developers had the freedom from regulation they enjoy in Houston, Portland would not have a problem with affordable housing. This argument needs to be examined more closely. New construction costs about the same everywhere, and the cost of renovating or maintaining older buildings is also similar from place to place. The price of land is only a small fraction of the cost of housing. Builders try not to buy land for more than 18 to 20 percent of the expected sale price for a house.[8] Twenty-five percent would be an upper limit, except in unusual places. The land cost per unit in a multiple dwelling will probably be less. There is undoubtedly a cost difference between land in Houston and land within Greater Portland, but removing the growth boundary would not magically make Portland's housing much more affordable.

Average housing costs are high in Portland, but about the same as they are in Denver, Sacramento, or the Washington, DC, metro area, and lower than in neighboring Seattle, and much lower than Los Angeles or San Diego, or super-high-cost San Francisco and Honolulu.[9] Demand for housing is strong in Portland: young people want to move there; older people want to retire there. It is a highly desirable place to live, and a good part of its livability is the result of careful planning, including the growth boundary. Finding affordable housing is a big problem in many parts of the United States. We come back to this issue in chapters 7 and 8.

Making Growth Boundaries Environmental-Protection Boundaries

Washington State and Tennessee also have urban growth boundary legislation, and there are growth boundaries in Miami-Dade County as well as in the Minneapolis–Saint Paul metro region. Some cities, such as Boulder, Colorado, have established growth boundaries inside their city limits. The growth boundary is an established legislative action that could be combined with GIS information and local environmental zoning to make the growth boundary an environmental-protection boundary. The legacy of Ebenezer Howard's greenbelt concept has made people think about growth boundaries as belts. But circular land reservations are not necessarily the best environmental protection policy. If growth boundaries were based on protecting land that should not be developed and permitting development in the most suitable locations, and if the land-preservation decisions were supported by the right utility and transportation plans, they could be both more flexible geographically and more effective in protecting farmland and other places that should not be destabilized by urbanization.

CHAPTER 4:

The Northeast Megaregion: Prototype for Balanced Transportation

Decisions about roads and highway routes are the de facto plans for US regions and megaregions, because property values are strongly affected by ease of access. New roads and highways in previously undeveloped areas inevitably unlock new investment. Reliance on cars and trucks spreads out development more than would be needed for the same number of houses, shops, and jobs if they were developed around a more balanced transportation system. Many people use highways for trips that would be more economic and efficient by trains or by rapid transit, and many local automobile trips could be made more efficiently and comfortably on foot or by bicycle—the challenge is to make this possible.

The Federal Highway Administration has predicted locations of peak highway congestion in 2040, as shown in figure 4-1. Most of the congestion coincides with the areas identified as the megaregions where much of the US population lives and works today, and which are expected to be even more dominant by 2040. The most congested areas on the map coincide with the evolving megaregions, showing how the highway system has been a major force in creating them. It also depicts

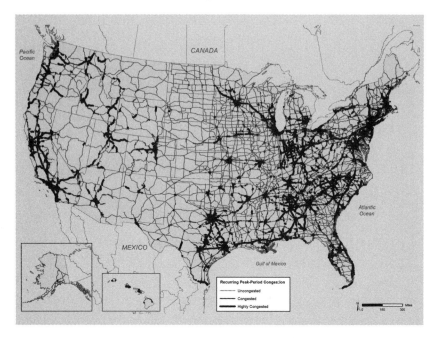

Figure 4-1: According to the US Department of Transportation, assuming no additional highways or widening projects, increases in truck and passenger vehicle traffic are forecast to expand areas of recurring peak-period congestion to 37 percent of the National Highway System in 2040 compared with 11 percent in 2007. This will slow traffic on twenty-one thousand miles of the highway system and create stop-and-go conditions on an additional forty thousand miles.

an unsustainable situation. A peak congestion period where traffic is effectively immobilized will take place on 37 percent of all highways by 2040, as opposed to 11 percent in 2007.[1]

This is a problem that can't be solved by widening highways or building more of them. It also cannot be solved by new automotive technology. Yes, computer-assisted cars and trucks could be in widespread use by 2040, but it is unlikely that this technology can make highways less congested, assuming the predicted number of vehicles remains the same. One human driver touching the brakes could cause such intense traffic to come to a standstill. And "self-driving" technology could very well increase the number of trips for each car or truck, if the vehicle is shared among multiple users all day, instead of being parked at a single destination. Even if congestion were to abate somewhat, the relatively free-moving highways will be likely to attract more vehicles, the same progression we can observe today.

Relying more on trains and less on highways and airplanes for inter-city travel, when the trips take less than two hours, could reduce one of the main sources of traffic and airline congestion. Regional transportation should offer affordable choices for everyone, and each transportation method should be designed for its optimal use: airline flights for long distances within and outside the region, upgraded train service on existing routes that interconnect regional centers, bus rapid transit (BRT) along development corridors when there is no rail transit, walking and bicycle paths for shorter distances. Right now the major missing component of a balanced megaregion transportation system is fast, dependable, frequent train service, the kind that is found in Europe as well as in Japan, Korea, and China.

People like the convenience and independence of their cars, and automobile ownership continues to go up, even in countries with excellent, balanced transportation systems. So far, the use of ride-hailing services has not changed this trend.[2] Because relying on cars and trucks has built the huge inventory of development created in the United States since the 1940s, any design for improving transportation within megaregions has to consider the existing development pattern and the attachment that people have to driving. At the same time, the people who can't afford a car, or are too young or too old to drive, and live outside a metro area with a strong transit system have to rely on conventional bus routes—which are often held up by traffic and have infrequent service—or pay for a taxi, Uber, or Lyft.

The sharing economy and the eventual availability of self-driving or assisted driving are also part of the context for regional transportation design. More people will have access to their own private vehicle, which will make traffic congestion worse. There is also evidence that companies like Uber and Lyft (transportation network companies or TNCs) are adding to traffic congestion because drivers without passengers keep moving about seeking fares. In New York City as of 2016, as many riders were taking TNCs as taxicabs.[3] A recent study of traffic in San Francisco found that, between 2010 and 2016, weekday vehicle hours of delay increased by 62 percent compared to an estimate of 22 percent for the same four-year period without TNCs.[4]

Improved trains and transit are needed to provide alternatives to traffic congestion, and to alleviate congestion at airports. Realizing the potential of existing physical assets, such as rail lines already constructed or highway lanes as transit corridors using BRT, can be more effective than waiting for massive investments in European- or Japanese-style high-speed rail or even in new local rail transit. There are many transportation improvements that can be made incrementally to give a much better structure to the evolving megaregions.

The Northeast Megaregion as Transportation Prototype

The Northeast megaregion, which extends from Richmond, Virginia, to Portland, Maine, comes close to having the kind of balanced transportation system found in European countries, where there are passenger and freight networks that date back more than a century, modern highways, airports, but also good-quality rail service, although not at the speeds available on premium trains in Europe. The dominant cities in the megaregion—Boston, New York, Philadelphia, Baltimore, and Washington—all have commuter rail systems to their suburbs and rail rapid transit in their central areas. Each one has a major airport. All the cities in the megaregion are tied together by highways, principally I-95, but also other major roads. And, gradually, the rail connections among these cities have been improved so that train travel has become a preferred choice over flying and has had some effect on reducing driving between Northeast Corridor (NEC) destinations as well.

Travel time on these trains does not rival high-speed trains running on their own special tracks; they are more like the Deutsche Bahn Inter-City Express trains in Europe, which share the rail rights-of-way with freight trains and local transit. According to Amtrak's timetables, the trip from New York to Washington on Amtrak's Acela Express takes just under three hours; from New York to Boston, it takes about four hours. Amtrak has captured more than three-quarters of the passengers who might otherwise fly between New York and Washington, and more than half the passengers between New York and Boston. While it is not high-speed rail, it is fast-enough rail.

Fast-Enough Rail in the Northeast Megaregion

In August 2016, in the closing days of the Obama administration, Amtrak ordered twenty-eight new trains from Alstom, a French manufacturer of high-speed trains, to replace the twenty trains currently being used for Amtrak's Acela service between Boston and Washington. Some of the new trains are expected to be in service in 2021, with full replacement completed by the end of 2022. The trains are being built in Alstom factories in New York State. They are part of a $2.45 billion improvement program for the NEC, which also includes some right-of-way improvements, modifications to repair facilities to accommodate the new trains, and station improvements in New York, Baltimore, and Washington. The financing comes from the Federal Railroad Administration's Railroad Rehabilitation & Improvement Financing program. The loan will be repaid through projected revenue growth from increased ridership because of the new trains.[5]

Comfort, Convenience, and Reliability as Important as Speed: The new investment will bring some small improvements in train speeds, but the big change will be improved train frequency and capacity. Having eight more trains will permit Amtrak to offer Acela service every half hour during peak periods between New York and Washington, and every hour between New York and Boston. Each train can carry about a third more passengers than the previous Acela trains. The new cars will also be more comfortable, with wider seats, improved Wi-Fi, and better food service. They include technology that permits them to tilt as much as 7 degrees, so they can go faster around the curves of the NEC right-of-way. The older Acela trains can tilt 4 degrees. But both trains can go much faster than the current right-of-way permits.

Attaining the full potential of these trains requires dealing with a backlog of badly needed repairs that require billions of dollars in additional funding. Amtrak has also identified significant choke points that slow down all trains, including the need for a new tunnel in West Baltimore, a replacement bridge at a river crossing in New Jersey near New York City, and the construction of the long-delayed additional two-track tunnel under the Hudson River into Pennsylvania Station, plus rehabilitation of the existing tunnel. When complete, the Hudson Tunnel work will double the number of trains per hour that can cross between New Jersey and New York. Renovation of such choke points and the completion of necessary repairs will ultimately lead to faster service, and the new equipment is supposed to be more reliable as well.

Making Connections to Airports with Fast-Enough Trains: Integrating rail and air travel is an important objective of a balanced transportation system. Making good connections between trains and airports could reduce the number of short-distance flights and relieve airport congestion. Some flight and rail connections exist now in the NEC, and people do use them, but connections are not so quick or easy as several places in Europe, where—for example—you can get off a high-speed rail train at Frankfurt Airport and the terminal is just up an escalator or elevator. Some Amtrak trains, and local trains, have a stop near BWI, the Baltimore/Washington International Thurgood Marshall Airport, where there is shuttle bus service to the terminal. Some Amtrak trains stop at the Newark Liberty International Airport, one of New York metro region's three major airports, where passengers can board a people mover that takes them directly to their terminal.

The Amtrak–Newark Liberty connection is the closest to providing an experience comparable to what has long been possible at many airports in Europe, but the Acela and some long-distance trains do not stop there yet.

Development at Amtrak Stations Can Help Finance Better Train Service: Local rail connections within the Northeast megaregion are much more like their European counterparts than elsewhere in the United States. There is a robust network of transit and commuter connections at each of the five central Amtrak stations, not only to the central business district but also to residential neighborhoods in these cities and out to the suburbs. They also connect to some of the urban subcenters that have grown up around highway interchanges, so that it is possible, for example, to take the Washington Metro from Tysons in Virginia, with its forty-six million square feet of office and retail space, to Amtrak's Union Station in Washington, which is also the hub for commuter trains from Virginia and Maryland.

Amtrak has long sought to improve its finances by attracting development to the air rights over Amtrak station properties and their adjacent rail yards. Increases in passenger traffic are helping to make these plans possible. Building over train tracks is expensive: railway operations have to continue during construction, and the placement of supporting columns is constrained by the tracks. But transportation access confers value on station locations, and the tracks are large sites in one ownership, which is also attractive for development.

There are plans for developing fourteen acres over the tracks approaching Washington's Union Station, including 1.5 million square feet of office space, more than thirteen hundred residential units, five hundred hotel rooms, and a hundred thousand square feet of retail beyond what is already in the station building. In Baltimore there are plans for developing Amtrak properties adjacent to the Amtrak station. The most ambitious Amtrak plan is for the 30th Street Station in Philadelphia: eighteen million square feet on 175 acres of development over the tracks leading into the station. (See figure 4-2.)

Figure 4-2: A rendering by Skidmore, Owings & Merrill of potential development over the yards at the 30th Street Station in Philadelphia. The existing buildings of downtown Philadelphia are at the lower left of this rendering; the proposed development on Amtrak property is across the Schuylkill River toward the top of the image. As well as being a stop on Amtrak's busy Northeast Corridor, 30th Street Station is the hub of the Southeastern Pennsylvania Transportation Authority (SEPTA) Regional Rail system, including a rail connection to Philadelphia International Airport. It is also an access point for Interstate 76. The development sites are next to the campus of Drexel University, and only a few blocks from the University of Pennsylvania.

The air rights over Pennsylvania Station in New York City were redeveloped long ago, before Amtrak, and led to the destruction of the historic station building. The development over the Hudson Yards, which are adjacent to Pennsylvania Station but belong to the Metropolitan Transit Authority, not to Amtrak, includes more than eighteen million square feet of offices, apartments, and stores.

The historic James A. Farley Building, once the central post office next to the yards, is being renovated into a new station, where the centerpiece will be the Daniel P. Moynihan Train Hall. Senator Moynihan worked for many years to preserve and reuse the building, which was part of the original station complex and was designed by McKim, Mead & White, the architects of the demolished terminal.

Finally, in Boston, a new tower is proposed over Amtrak's tracks at historic South Station. Preservation laws would make it difficult to destroy Amtrak's historic station buildings today; they are being renovated to remain the important civic gateways that have always been their purpose.

Faster Trains by 2040

The Federal Railroad Administration's NEC Future Program is a strategy to offer faster service in the Northeast Corridor by 2040 by making major track improvements and possibly building a new rail segment for a more direct route from New York to Boston, while keeping all the existing lines. The plan is to take fifty minutes off the New York–Boston trip and thirty-five minutes from the New York–Washington trip. The plan includes having long-distance and fast trains stop at BWI, Philadelphia Airport, and Newark Liberty Airport. Amtrak has already attracted a majority of people who might otherwise travel by air, and will accelerate this trend by greatly increasing train–air connections. The 2040 improvements in travel times will also make trains more competitive with driving, although taking a train is still likely to be more expensive, especially for families. However, the track improvements will also benefit other, slower Amtrak services, with more competitive prices, which will also have shorter travel times.

The costs of safeguarding the NEC tracks from sea level rise is not included in current Amtrak plans, but by 2040 there are likely to be major vulnerabilities for tracks along the Delaware River, crossing the New Jersey Meadowlands, and along Amtrak routes that run near Long Island Sound through New York, Connecticut, and Rhode Island. It is possible that raising the tracks to defend against rising sea levels can be incorporated into other track improvements, and an inland route through New England that is already being studied might be made longer to avoid exposure along the shore.

Freight Trains Can Limit the Speed of Passenger Trains: Amtrak owns much of the right-of-way in the NEC, sharing it with commuter rail but relatively few freight trains. In the rest of the country, the rail lines through the megaregions are owned by major freight railways. By statute, Amtrak trains are supposed to receive preferential access to all tracks, with a few legislated exceptions, regardless of ownership. Amtrak currently pays these railroads $142 million each year for using their tracks and other resources needed for it to operate.

In 2018, Amtrak began issuing a report card for the big freight railways, based on the number of delays caused to Amtrak trains that had to wait until a freight train passed. Canadian Pacific received an A; BNSF a B+; Union Pacific a B−; CSX received a C; and Norfolk Southern and Canadian National both were given a failing grade. A failing grade means all Amtrak trains on the routes operated by these two companies are delayed an average of one hour and forty minutes waiting for freight trains, and many Amtrak trains are delayed as long as three hours and twelve minutes on these routes by freight trains interfering with passenger trains.

The freight railways, which are all profitable private companies, were required to give Amtrak priority on their tracks in exchange for Amtrak's taking over their money-losing passenger services in 1971. Sharing the tracks requires an intricate schedule. The freight trains are meant to arrive at sidings at predetermined places so that the passenger trains can go by. The Amtrak trains have an obligation to pass by on time so that the freight train can resume its journey. Amtrak has been able to sustain this arrangement with some of the freight lines, but not all.[6]

Lessons for Other Megaregions from the Northeast Corridor

What are the components of a balanced transportation system?

Complete Highway and Road Networks: Highways have facilitated the growth of the Northeast megaregion and will remain essential, as cars and trucks will continue to be primary forms of transportation. All the megaregions have such road systems, although they also all have many places that need repair and improvement.

Transit and Commuter Rail Systems: These networks have their own exclusive rights-of-way, and provide significant alternatives to driving in all five of the major cities in the Northeast megaregion. The commuter trains and rail transit in Boston, New York City, and Philadelphia are based on legacy systems from the early twentieth century. However, the Washington Metro system, which extends into Maryland and Virginia, is as comprehensive as the three legacy systems and opened in 1976. It now includes six lines and functions as both transit and commuter rail. There are also additional commuter rail services to Union Station from Maryland and Virginia. Baltimore has a single Metro Subway line, which opened in 1983, and a Link transit system consisting of light-rail lines, the first lines opening in 1992, integrated with an extensive bus system on local streets.

Container Ports and Freight Railways: Loading shipping containers on freight trains, rather than on long-haul trucks, reduces congestion on highways. These operations are profitable and are supported by private investment. The New York City region has a major container operation at Port Newark. Boston, Philadelphia, and Baltimore also have container ports for more local freight traffic.

Fast-Enough Trains: Sharing a right-of-way can deliver most of the advantages of higher-speed trains, if service is frequent and comfortable. However, the freight lines that own the tracks need to integrate their timetables with frequent passenger trains to avoid the long delays created by freight trains that fall behind schedule. True high-speed rail trains would be an even better alternative, if they can be funded and built. For train services to reach their full potential, stations in major cities need to be part of a complete network of local transit and commuter rail.

Direct Connections from Trains to Airports: Airport–rail connections can attract additional rail passengers transferring to a train for short segments of a trip, as does happen at some European airports. If these connections are possible, airlines may be able to offer fewer short-haul flights, which can reduce airport congestion and eliminate—or decrease the need for—expensive and disruptive new runways.

Real Estate Development: Developers can be attracted to major long-distance train terminals that have good connections to commuter rail and transit. Development revenues could help support rail-service capital and operational costs.

CHAPTER 5:

Progress Toward Fast-Enough Trains in Megaregions

The addition of frequent fast-enough train service in the Northeast megaregion has attracted a majority of airline passengers who would otherwise make short flights within the region and, along with local commuter train and transit systems, has taken cars off local highways. The main highways are still congested, and the congestion is still predicted to become worse, but an infrastructure that permits choices is in place. Continued improvements in train travel times and better integration of air and rail services will draw more passengers from planes and cars.

Upgrading existing intercity train services to the level of the Acela service available on Amtrak along the East Coast, and having these trains connect to airports to reduce airport congestion from short-distance flights, would redesign the development of emerging megaregions. Unlike high-speed trains, which require land acquisition for expensive and intrusive elevated guideways, rail rights-of-way at ground level are already available.

Using conventional technology like the Acela for rail service from Birmingham, Alabama, to Atlanta, Georgia—for example—would cut the train trip from more than four hours to less than two, although making this change would require electrification of the route as well as track improvements. As on the Acela route, these kinds of travel times make it much easier to go from one city to another for a meeting and be back the same day, and can help integrate the economies of cities within the same megaregion. The route could also connect the two airports as well as the downtown rail terminals. While this initiative might take some cars off the highways, an important effect would be to reduce the demand for flights between—in this example—Atlanta and Birmingham. These kinds of connections can reduce the congestion at airports and eliminate the need for costly and controversial new runways or runway extensions.

Designs for an integrated airport and intercity rail system could become an organizing factor for the evolving megaregions. Downtowns and other locations selected as transit hubs can be connected to this system. Bus rapid transit (BRT) can be fitted into existing roadways and permit higher densities along what would then become transit corridors. The well-known benefit of transit-oriented design is that it supports compact walkable communities. Again, the transit probably would not have a major effect on regional automobile use, but it would support major development corridors that could take some of the development pressure off the urban fringe. Current regional designs, such as the Helsinki 2050 Plan and the Stockholm 2040 Plan, accommodate predicted regional growth by creating corridors of more intensive development along highways and roadways that go through existing areas, with new investment supported by rail transit and busways.

Private Investment in Fast Trains

Advocates for passenger rail service in the United States have assumed that the construction and property acquisition costs would have to be borne by government, and operations would not earn enough money to be attractive to a private business. Today, for the first time in many years, there are private investors who are prepared to build and fund passenger rail transit—if the travel time, using the best available technology, is not more than two to three hours between key cities, and the cities are within megaregions. Perhaps the example of Jeff Bezos guiding Amazon from major losses to both dominance and profitability has made investors more comfortable with financing passenger rail companies with high front-end costs and a potentially long wait for a return on investment.

Improved passenger rail service will not balance transportation in a megaregion by itself. In addition to the complete highway and road networks that all megaregions have, they also need transit with its own rights-of-way, commuter rail systems, direct connections from trains to airports, and freight railways—as well as a container port and freight connections in megaregions that have ports. The private investment plans for railroads all include development at station locations. The real estate potential at station locations can be a means of financing train and transit improvements, a validation that a balanced transportation system is attracting development to these central locations.

The Florida megaregion is the first to see significant private investment in long-distance trains. Trains can take Florida closer to having a balanced system comparable to the Northeast because of previous investments in transit and airports that will help support a new privately funded passenger rail system. There are plans for new privately funded passenger services in the Texas and Southern California megaregions as well.

The Off-Again, On-Again Story of Florida's Passenger Rail

The Florida megaregion, which includes cities from Miami northward on the southeast Florida coast and then extends westward to include Orlando and Tampa, has population concentrations comparable to those in the Northeast megaregion. The first attempt to create a new passenger rail system took place in 2000, when voters in Florida approved a constitutional amendment mandating a high-speed rail line:

"To reduce traffic congestion and provide alternatives to the traveling public, it is hereby declared to be in the public interest that a high speed ground transportation system . . . link the five largest urban areas of the State . . . and provide for access to existing air and ground transportation facilities and services."[1]

This is a good prescription for balancing the transportation system within the Florida megaregion. A newly created state agency completed preliminary engineering work on the routes, but the amendment was repealed by the voters in 2004 after opposition by Republican governor Jeb Bush and a campaign that stressed high estimated costs. In 2009, as part of the federal government's financial stimulus package after the Great Recession, Florida was invited to apply for funding to build the first link of a high-speed rail line between Tampa and Orlando. The Florida project got on the Obama administration's list as "shovel ready," because of preliminary engineering and an environmental impact statement completed in 2005.

Under Governor Charlie Crist, a Republican, Florida pursued the funding, including seeking and receiving the legislature's approval to fund and build SunRail, a local commuter train in the Orlando region to connect with the high-speed intercity rail line that was considered a critical part of Florida's application for federal funds. The federal government awarded Florida $2.4 billion toward building a high-speed rail line between Downtown Tampa and Orlando International Airport, but in 2011, newly elected governor Rick Scott, also a Republican, refused to accept the funds, to the dismay of business leaders in Florida who were strong advocates for the project.

Governor Scott said he acted because the state could be stuck with paying for cost overruns and would end up subsidizing continual operating deficits. Despite Governor Scott's certainty that railroads always lose money, a private company, Florida East Coast Railway (FEC), announced in 2012 that it would operate a fast passenger service on its own tracks, in addition to its freight services. Its parent company, Florida East Coast Industries, is in turn part of the Fortress Investment Group. At the time, it owned the tracks and right-of-way from Jacksonville to Miami. Its plan is to extend service northward from Miami on the FEC tracks to Cocoa, near Port Canaveral on the Florida East Coast, and then construct new tracks following a highway westward to Orlando's airport. Passengers began traveling on the line, originally named All Aboard America, between Miami, Fort Lauderdale, and West Palm Beach in the winter of 2018. A link to Tampa along the Interstate 4 right-of-way, stopping at the Disney attractions, would be the final part of the line completed. These last portions of the line will be new, but the trains will also continue to share the FEC tracks, which have since been sold to a Mexican conglomerate. Like Amtrak's Acela service, it will be fast-enough rail.

Fortress Investment Group was acquired in 2017 by the Japanese investment firm SoftBank; then, in November 2018, its rail subsidiary, Brightline, formed a strategic partnership with Virgin Trains USA, part of the group of businesses controlled by British entrepreneur Richard Branson. The Brightline trains will now be called Virgin Trains, as Virgin is a far-better-known brand.

Virgin Trains USA has filed an initial public offering registration statement with the US Securities and Exchange Commission, which says: "We own and operate an express passenger rail system connecting major population centers in Florida, with plans to expand operations further in Florida, Las Vegas and elsewhere in North America. We are the first new major private passenger intercity railroad in the United States in over a century, and we believe our business represents a scalable model for twenty-first century passenger travel in North America."[2]

The Virgin Trains USA prospectus identifies other places where the company may consider building and operating high-speed rail service, all parts of lines designated by the Federal Railroad Administration as future high-speed rail routes that coincide closely with the areas identified as emerging megaregions. (See figure 5-1.)

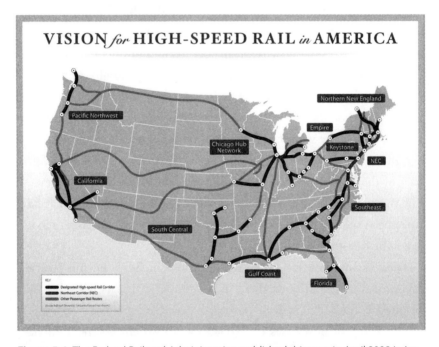

Figure 5-1: The Federal Railroad Administration published this map in April 2009 in its report titled *Vision for High-Speed Rail in America*. President Obama allocated $8 billion to begin implementing this vision as part of the American Recovery and Reinvestment Act, and proposed an annual grant program of $1 billion in continuing funding. The proposed high-speed lines coincide with the emerging megaregions. While the original funding proposals failed for various reasons, high-speed, or at least fast-enough, trains on these routes are essential to managing optimal growth in the megaregions.

According to the Virgin Trains USA prospectus, it will use existing infrastructure to plan, obtain permits, and build new rail service significantly faster and cheaper than alternative express passenger rail projects that require new rights-of-way. It plans to concentrate on rail segments of two hundred to three hundred miles that connect large population centers and have high—and increasing—volumes of travelers. The company identifies Houston–Dallas, Atlanta–Charlotte, Chicago–Saint Louis, Los Angeles–San Diego, Portland–Seattle–Vancouver, San Antonio–Austin–Dallas, and Houston–San Antonio–Dallas as potential future routes.

The long-distance service that Virgin Trains will offer between Miami and Orlando will complete a balanced transportation system comparable to what is available in the Northeast megaregion. The new Virgin Trains station in Miami is right in the center of downtown, next to both the Metromover—a free, automated people mover that connects downtown destinations—and a Metrorail station, which includes a line with direct access to Miami International Airport. It is also a short taxi ride to the cruise ship terminal in the Port of Miami. In Fort Lauderdale the station is downtown, close to the regional bus station and a short taxi ride from both the airport and the cruise ship terminal. It would be possible to add a station at the Fort Lauderdale airport. In West Palm Beach the station is also in the center of the downtown, and the airport is not far away.

There is also the Tri-Rail commuter line serving these three cities on a different track, providing a slower, lower-cost alternative, but serving many intermediate stops, offering shuttle connections to the West Palm Beach and Fort Lauderdale airports, and going directly to the Miami airport instead of downtown.

Amtrak also serves the same megaregion, and there are frequent correspondence points between Amtrak and Tri-Rail. Tri-Rail offers trains every twenty minutes at peak periods, and no less than once an hour at other times. Amtrak trains head inland north of West Palm Beach. It is possible to travel from Miami to Orlando on Amtrak, but it takes a long time. There is a choice of two long-distance trains that make this trip: one is scheduled to take five hours and eleven minutes between the two stations, and the other takes seven hours and twenty-six minutes. Amtrak shares these tracks with the freight company CSX. Amtrak gives CSX a C on its report card for shared tracks, meaning delays are likely.

Virgin Trains plans to offer service between downtown Miami and Orlando International Airport in approximately three hours. From the Orlando airport, it should be possible to make a connection from the Virgin Trains airport station to SunRail's Sand Lake Road station for local trips in the Orlando region, including downtown. When the Virgin Trains route is extended to Tampa, a potential stop at the SunRail station will be on the way from the airport to the I-4 right-of-way, the planned route to Tampa. Three hours between Miami and Orlando is faster than driving on the Florida Turnpike, a toll road where the estimated travel time for this trip is about three and a half hours, and faster than driving the often-congested I-95, which could take about four hours or more.

The fastest flights from Miami to Orlando take a little over an hour, but check-in is at least an hour before flight time—an hour and half if checking baggage, and assuming no long lines for check-in or security, and no air-traffic delays. A Japanese high-speed train could make the Miami–Orlando trip in about two hours. A comparable high-speed service is not likely to be available in Florida. If you are connecting from one airplane to another, flying from Miami to Orlando makes the best sense. From elsewhere in the Miami region, you will probably save time spending three hours going from Miami to Orlando on Virgin Trains USA's new, fast-enough train, especially when the connection is completed to the local SunRail service.

As soon as the link to the Orlando airport is complete, the Florida megaregion will have a much more balanced transportation system, which will start uniting the tourist visits and the local economies of its individual cities. The system will be enhanced when the direct connection to the Disney attractions is completed and the rail line goes on to Downtown Tampa, passing close to the Tampa airport. The unanswered question is whether the fast-enough trains will be profitable enough for a private company to keep them going.

Balancing Transportation in Other Megaregions

Some other megaregions are relatively well prepared to take advantage of improved train service. They have existing local transit and passenger rail to supply the missing links to highways, air connections, and ports. Improvements in the Northeast megaregion and in Florida, and private proposals for Dallas–Houston and Las Vegas–Victorville, California, are indications that the United States may soon be operating high-speed— or fast-enough—services that link key parts of some megaregions. There is also California's high-speed rail system, intended to be as fast as Japanese or European trains, and totally constructed with government funds. While such investments are routine government expenditures in Europe and Asia, the California experience is demonstrating that this kind of high-speed rail may not be a viable alternative in the United States.

California's Long-Distance High-Speed Rail, an Expensive Mistake? One hundred nineteen miles of high-speed rail tracks, designed like the Japanese or Chinese systems as an elevated, exclusive right-of-way, are being built in California. The map from the California High-Speed Rail Authority, figure 5-2, shows the whole proposed phase-one route in white, with future extensions to Sacramento and to San Diego. The segment under construction is in the Central Valley. Amtrak already runs eight conventional trains a day along almost the same route from Merced to Bakersfield. The trip takes just under two hours.

More difficult connections through mountain ranges to San Francisco and Los Angeles remain in an indeterminate future, as Governor Gavin Newsom has put the plans for these connections on hold. Parts

Figure 5-2: An ambitious plan to link San Francisco to Los Angeles via a high-speed train comparable to trains in Japan and China is shown by the white line on this map. Future extensions would link north to Sacramento and south to San Diego. A $30 billion section in the Central Valley is actually under construction. Unfortunately, there are no funds to connect to either San Francisco or Los Angeles. Former governor Jerry Brown placed a big bet that his successors would have to fund the rest of the project if he made the commitment to build the less challenging central section. His successor, Governor Gavin Newsom, has put the rest of the project on hold.

of these connecting routes would use conventional tracks also used by other trains. If the line is ever completed, the high-speed trip from San Francisco to Los Angeles would be about three hours, using trains that can attain 220 miles per hour on the central segment, but more conventional speeds in urban areas at either end. The completed line would link the Bay Area megaregion with the Southern California megaregion.

The high-speed line's share of funding under the American Recovery and Reinvestment Act (the Obama stimulus plan) has been $2.55 billion,[3] some of it redirected from other states where the governors had refused the money. Most of the rest of the funding, which is expected to be around $30 billion for the initial segment, has been from a State of California bond issue and other state programs, with some additional matching grants from the federal government. Completing the system will require major additional funding sources. The ultimate cost of the more-than-520-mile San Francisco–Los Angeles system in phase one, plus another 280 miles for later extensions to San Diego and Sacramento, is still unknown, but is expected to be more than $100 billion. The problem with the initial route through California's Central Valley is the lack of potential passengers for the first completed segment, as the Central Valley is primarily agricultural.

There is a question whether it will even make sense to operate the high-speed segment when it is completed, rather than just continuing to operate the existing Amtrak trains on the parallel route. The decision will depend on whether trains purchased for the high-speed segment can operate on conventional tracks as well, making it possible to switch from high-speed rail service to Amtrak service and continue on to Oakland, across the bay from San Francisco. Amtrak only runs a connecting bus service to Los Angeles from the end of the high-speed line in Bakersfield.

The California High-Speed Rail line was planned to run directly from San Francisco south to San Jose on Caltrain tracks on the west side of the bay. The route from there would require going through Pacheco Pass in the Diablo Range to connect to the segment in the Central Valley. From Bakersfield, the high-speed line will need to traverse another mountain range through Tehachapi Pass and then will need to go through or under the San Gabriel Mountains to bring the trains into Downtown Los Angeles. Former governor Jerry Brown and other state officials placed a big bet on long-distance high-speed rail travel. They assumed that, if they build the central segment, other state administrations will have to find a way to fund and build the connections to San Francisco and Los Angeles. In retrospect, the $30 billion expended on the central segment could have gone a long way toward funding fast-enough trains, like the Acela, on Amtrak routes within the Bay Area and Los Angeles megaregions.

The Bay Area Megaregion: The Bay Area megaregion is relatively small, not much larger than some big metropolitan areas, and already has most of the components of a well-balanced transportation system. The Bay Area Rapid Transit system connects many parts of the region and provides direct access to both the San Francisco and Oakland airports via people movers. There are Caltrain commuter rail lines serving San Francisco along the San Francisco Peninsula; and Amtrak's Capital Corridor trains offer frequent service along the East Bay between Oakland and San Jose. San Francisco has its Muni Metro for local transit, as well as the famous cable cars and heritage streetcars. There are ferries providing frequent passenger service. But there are gaps in the transportation systems within the Bay Area megaregion. Money spent on high-speed rail in the California's Central Valley could have funded an Acela level of service for trains running on both sides of the bay, like the route from Oakland to Sacramento and the existing route from San Francisco to Los Angeles, plus significant improvements to local transit service.

The Southern California Megaregion: The Southern California megaregion is much larger than the Bay Area, extending at least from

Santa Barbara through Los Angeles to San Diego. A privately funded high-speed rail initiative is likely to extend this megaregion across the desert to Las Vegas. Virgin Trains has acquired a company called Xpress-West, which has completed plans and permits for passenger rail service on trains capable of attaining 150 miles an hour between Las Vegas and Victorville, California, along a right-of-way to be constructed in the I-15 highway corridor. The 180-mile trip will probably take less than an hour and a half, as opposed to a more-than-three-hour drive now. Victorville, on the other side of the mountainous Angeles National Forest from the Greater Los Angeles region, is within about a forty-five-minute drive from many Los Angeles destinations. A future phase would extend the line westward to Palmdale, and then south to the center of Los Angeles. The XpressWest trains between Victorville and Las Vegas are designed so that they can also run on California's high-speed rail line, should its link to Los Angeles be completed.

The Southern California megaregion already has an extensive commuter rail system, Metrolink. Figure 5-3 shows the Metrolink rail lines. There is also a rail and busway transit system, the Los Angeles Metro, which connects to all the Metrolink lines at Union Station. The Los Angeles Metro began construction in 1990 and now consists of two heavy-rail routes (conventional rail transit), four light-rail routes (streetcars on their own rights-of-way), and two busways (buses running on exclusive rights-of-way). There are long-range plans to connect Metrolink to the Las Vegas XpressWest train.

The Los Angeles megaregion also has connections to longer-distance passenger rail north to Santa Barbara and south to San Diego, but most trips are not fast enough to be effective competition with planes and cars. Amtrak (the line nearest the water in figure 5-3) runs frequent Pacific Surfliner trains from Los Angeles to San Diego, almost one an hour. However, the trip takes about three hours. The distance is about the same as Philadelphia to Washington, DC. A Northeast Regional

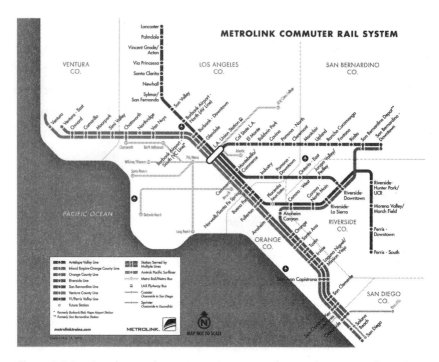

Figure 5-3: Los Angeles now has an extensive system of regional trains as well as rail and busway transit. Amtrak is the line on the map closest to the water. Amtrak already runs trains from Santa Barbara to Los Angeles and from Los Angeles to San Diego. Improved speed and frequency on these routes, up to the level of the Acela service on the East Coast, would help coordinate and manage the growth of the megaregion. The proposed XpressWest high-speed rail route to Las Vegas could eventually be connected to the regional rail system. Unfortunately, none of these routes make good connections to the megaregion's airports.

Amtrak train makes the Philadelphia–Washington trip in about two hours; the Acela Express in an hour and forty minutes. Reducing the Los Angeles–San Diego rail trip to an hour and forty minutes should be fast enough to capture a substantial share of air passengers between both destinations, and even some drivers.

Amtrak also runs five trains daily each way between Los Angeles and Santa Barbara, as well as the daily through train that eventually connects to San Francisco. The scheduled train time between Los Angeles and Santa Barbara is a little under three hours. The distance is about the same as Philadelphia to Baltimore. A Northeast Regional Amtrak train makes the Philadelphia–Baltimore trip in an hour and fifteen minutes; the Acela service makes the trip in just over an hour. Fast-enough trains comparable to what is available on the East Coast would make a big difference in travel times, bringing all the cities in the Southern California megaregion much closer together and helping to balance their transportation systems.

Upgrading the existing trains linking Santa Barbara to Los Angeles and on to San Diego at the level of service provided by the Acela could have been funded with a fraction of the money being expended building high-speed rail in the Central Valley. Service from Los Angeles to San Diego is one of the routes mentioned in the Virgin Trains prospectus as a possible high-speed train investment; it is also promised as one of the last extensions of the high-speed rail system. Once in San Diego, there are three light-rail lines (called the San Diego Trolley) that connect to the Amtrak terminal. One line goes all the way to San Ysidro, near the Mexican border.

Train and transit connections to the Los Angeles airports are conspicuously missing today, and there are no future plans to improve these connections. There is a bus between a Metrolink station and Ontario International Airport, way east of downtown in San Bernardino County. A sort-of connection runs between a Metrolink station and Long Beach Airport, south of Los Angeles.

There is a free shuttle bus from Los Angeles International Airport (LAX) to the Aviation/LAX stop on the Metro Green Line, which in turn connects to the other Metro lines and to the Metro hub at Union Station and all the rail lines shown in figure 5-3. However, these connections are far from seamless. High-speed rail is planned to arrive, like Amtrak, at Union Station downtown, nowhere near the main airport or any of the other airports in the region. Passengers seeking to connect to LAX from Union Station via Metro, if it remains as it is now, will find it has many stops, requires changing to a different line and the airport station is a long way from the terminals. There are plans to replace the shuttle bus with a people mover.

The connection between airport and passenger rail is better in San Diego. There is a bus connection with fifteen-minute headways from San Diego International Airport to the railroad depot downtown, which is not far away and also connects to the San Diego Trolley system.

The Southern California megaregion is some of the way toward achieving a balanced transportation system, although it still needs faster train connections from San Diego through to Santa Barbara, which are technically feasible but are not funded. An extension of the Metro Green Line into LAX would draw more airplane passengers into the transit system and out of cars, taxis, and buses, which all need to use the congested highways. But direct links between airport and long-distance train look to be missing for a long time, unlike the connections built into the Florida megaregion and planned for the Northeast megaregion.

The Texas Megaregion: What is considered to be the Texas megaregion is a group of metropolitan areas separated by long stretches of ranch and agricultural land and connected by three interstate highways: I-10, I-35, and I-45. The three highway corridors form a triangle, and the region is sometimes called the Texas Triangle, which includes Dallas–Fort Worth, Houston, San Antonio, and Austin. The existing rail service in Texas does not support a megaregion. Amtrak has one long-distance train a day, the Texas Eagle, which runs from Chicago to Los Angeles. It stops at Dallas, Fort Worth, Austin, and San Antonio. From Dallas to San Antonio on this train takes more than ten hours. The Sunset Limited Amtrak long-distance service runs from New Orleans to Los Angeles, stopping at Houston and San Antonio. It only runs every other day; the segment between Houston and San Antonio takes just under six hours; and the hours are inconvenient.

Amtrak does not operate between Dallas and Houston. However, Texas Central is a company formed to build and operate a train service on the approximately 240-mile Houston–Dallas route, which is also mentioned by Virgin Trains USA in its prospectus. Texas Central plans to use an eight-car version of the trains developed for the Japanese Shinkansen lines. Unlike Virgin Trains, which says it will primarily use existing tracks, the Shinkansen trains require a separate track system to attain their designed speeds, which are projected to make the travel time between Dallas and Houston less than ninety minutes, with departures every thirty minutes during peak periods each day, and every hour during off-peak periods. Texas Central has mapped out a proposed route, and is negotiating with property owners, and explaining plans to other property owners who will be affected by the raised track system. Under Texas law, the company says, railways can exercise eminent domain to acquire rights-of-way needed for their service. Texas Central has named Renfe, the operating company for high-speed rail lines in Spain, to manage its train service and has signed a design-build agreement with a construction company. Texas Central plans to raise the estimated $15 to $18 billion needed and says that it will not seek state or federal grants for construction or operations. The Japan Bank for International Cooperation has conducted a feasibility study of the project and may be a source of financing.

In Houston the Texas Central terminal will be the site of the Northwest Mall, which closed in 2017. There are good highway connections to the Interstate 610 inner ring road, Interstate 10, and Highway 290, but passengers arriving on the train will need to rent a car or take a taxi to their actual destination. The Melbourne/North Lindale stop on the Houston METRORail Red Line is about seven miles away. A link to that station would give rail passengers access to Houston's downtown and many other destinations, but it is a big gap, and there are no plans to make the connection. The Northwest train terminal is a long way from either of Houston's two airports, so there is little prospect for connecting high-speed rail to long-distance flights.

The site chosen for the Texas Central station in Dallas has better potential connections than the Houston terminus. The Dallas station will be on the Trinity riverfront just southwest of a major downtown highway intersection. Dallas's Kay Bailey Hutchinson Convention Center is on the other side of this massive interchange, within people mover range, and there is a Dallas Area Rapid Transit (DART) station at the convention center. Once on DART, it is possible to change to the DART Orange Line service to Dallas–Fort Worth International Airport. DART also connects to the nearby Dallas Union Station, where there is hourly train service between Dallas and Fort Worth. These trains also stop near the Dallas–Fort Worth airport, although a long way from the terminals.

Both Texas Central terminal locations have the potential to become high-density development sites, which could possibly help pay for the rail line.

The designated high-speed rail corridor for Texas on the Federal Railroad Administration map shown in figure 5-1 does not include Houston, but runs from San Antonio through Austin to Dallas and then on to Oklahoma City and Tulsa. The map also shows a branch high-speed corridor from Dallas to Little Rock. The distances are long for fast-enough trains to be fully effective, although the Virgin Trains USA prospectus, which is based on using shared existing tracks, mentions the route from San Antonio to Dallas, and also suggests connecting to Houston.

If faster trains are built, cities along the route will need to make major transit improvements to gain full benefits from the service. San Antonio does not have a transit system with its own rights-of-way, although there is a plan to build busways and possibly some rail connections by 2040.

Austin has a single commuter rail line, Capital MetroRail; otherwise, all transit is by bus in shared rights-of-way. The Texas megaregion is a long way from having a balanced transportation system, although the high-speed link between Dallas and Houston would be a good start. Dallas is the Texas city best positioned to relate to high-speed rail connections.

Megaregions around Chicago: Chicago, like Paris, has rail lines coming in to separate stations from several directions, so Chicago can be considered the hub of several linear megaregions radiating out from the city. Figure 5-4 shows the regional Amtrak rail corridors radiating out from Chicago.

The route north from Chicago to Milwaukee is only eighty-five miles, and it runs through a region where urban areas are close together. Democratic governor Jim Doyle secured $810 million for new trains and track improvements for this line, as well as funding an extension on to the Wisconsin State Capitol in Madison, all part of the 2009 stimulus package. After Republican governor Scott Walker took office in 2011, he refused the money. Amtrak continues to offer seven trains a day between Milwaukee and Chicago, and the trip takes about an hour and a half. There is a stop at the Milwaukee airport, but unfortunately, the route misses Chicago's O'Hare International Airport by about five miles. O'Hare is reachable from downtown Chicago via the Chicago Transit Authority, which has a station at the airport, but that is not the same as having a direct connection from one of the nation's busiest airports to the national rail system. Chicago's Metra commuter rail system has a train service with stops close to O'Hare. Metra offers a train that goes as far as Kenosha, Wisconsin—but not all the way to Milwaukee. Going on from Milwaukee to Minneapolis–Saint Paul is more than three hundred miles through farmland, and is really a long-distance route outside the megaregion. Amtrak currently offers train service once a day between Milwaukee and Minneapolis on its Empire Builder train; the trip takes at least eight hours.

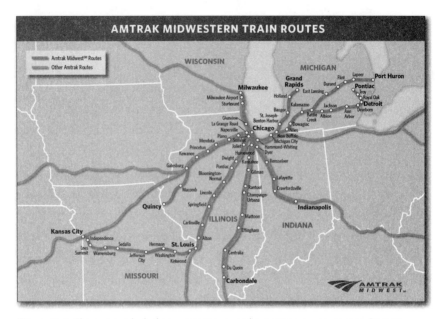

Figure 5-4: Chicago is a hub that connects several emerging megaregions. Progress toward fast-enough trains is being made on the routes from Chicago to Detroit and from Chicago to Saint Louis. The Amtrak route from Chicago to Milwaukee misses Chicago's O'Hare International Airport by about five miles. Connecting O'Hare into a regional system of fast-enough trains could reduce some of the demand for short flights, easing congestion at one of the nation's busiest airports.

There is a plan being implemented for incremental improvements to the route from Chicago southward to Saint Louis for trains that can attain 110 miles per hour. The 284-mile trip would then take four and a half hours, saving about an hour from current speeds, similar to the best potential driving time between the two cities. There are currently five trains a day. Flight times from O'Hare to Saint Louis are only about an hour and twenty minutes, but then there is the need to arrive early at the airport so that the airport-to-airport trip is about three hours, at best. There are two trains a day between Saint Louis and Kansas City, about the same distance as between Saint Louis and Chicago. The trip takes five and a half hours, and there are no current plans to speed it up. Neither trip will be like the fast-enough trains that support the Northeast and Florida megaregions.

A third potential megaregion transportation corridor is the connection between Chicago and Detroit via Kalamazoo. Amtrak runs three trains a day in each direction along this 281-mile route, where the trip currently takes about five hours. Amtrak owns a substantial part of the right-of-way, and the State of Michigan used US government stimulus funds to purchase much of the remaining trackage along the route. The tracks are being upgraded to permit maximum train speeds of 110 miles per hour, which will be faster train service, but not the frequency and speed of trains in the Northeast and Florida megaregions. However, most of the route is in the state of Michigan, which means that the State could continue to finance further upgrades of track speed and train frequency. There are plans for high-speed rail from Toronto to London, Ontario, through a Canadian megaregion. This route could be extended to Windsor, Ontario, across the Detroit River, so a future fast-enough line from Chicago to Toronto might one day be possible. Making these connections could be highly beneficial for the Detroit region.

Other corridors radiating from Chicago in figure 5-4 do not show many signs of progress toward higher-speed rail. The State of Ohio under Democratic governor Ted Strickland applied for, and received, $400 million of the 2009 federal stimulus funds to improve the train connections from Cincinnati through Columbus to Cleveland—but Republican governor John Kasich gave the money back after he was elected in 2010.

The Southeast Megaregion: The Southeast megaregion extends from Birmingham, Alabama, through Atlanta to Charlotte, North Carolina, and then on to North Carolina's Raleigh–Durham region. Virgin Trains has identified Atlanta to Charlotte as a potential fast-enough rail route. The rail line would pass close to Charlotte Douglas International

Airport, but unfortunately not by Atlanta's airport, although the Metropolitan Atlanta Rapid Transit Authority stops near the Amtrak station and does connect directly into the airport terminal. There are several Amtrak long-distance trains that wend their way through this region, all of them one train a day in each direction and none of them fast. The tracks are there, however, and it would be possible to design a service that started by linking Atlanta and Charlotte and then went on to connect southward to Birmingham and north and east to Raleigh.

The Pacific Northwest Megaregion: Amtrak's Cascades service connects the cities of the Pacific Northwest megaregion, which extends from Eugene, Oregon, through Portland, Tacoma, and Seattle and on to Vancouver, British Columbia. The entire trip on a through train takes ten and a half hours, but the service includes four daily round trips between Portland and Seattle (three and a half hours each way), two daily round trips between Seattle and Vancouver (five hours), and two daily round trips between Eugene and Portland (just under three hours).

When there are no traffic delays, it is sometimes possible to drive on Interstate 5 from Portland to Seattle in under three hours, saving some of the time it takes on the train. Incremental improvements, designed to produce results comparable to service in the Northeast megaregion, could bring the travel time on a train between Seattle and Portland to less than three hours. While the air travel time between the two cities is only about an hour, the complications with taking a plane make taking a faster train a very competitive choice. There is a transit connection to Portland International Airport from Downtown Portland, and the train route passes close to the Seattle–Tacoma and Vancouver airports. Seattle has a good BRT system, and Vancouver has its SkyTrain rapid transit.

The long-range prospects for balancing the transportation system in the Pacific Northwest may be favorable. Portland–Seattle and Seattle–Vancouver are among the routes targeted by Virgin Trains USA in its prospectus.

Front Range Megaregion, Gulf Coast Megaregion, Arizona Megaregion: The Rocky Mountain Rail Authority commissioned a high-speed rail feasibility study of the north–south I-25 corridor from Cheyenne, Wyoming, through Denver to Trinidad, Colorado (south of Pueblo), and the east–west I-70 corridor across the Rocky Mountains from Denver to Grand Junction. The study was completed in 2010, and early estimates placed costs on the order of $22 billion. The east–west route has excited the most interest but is also the most challenging because of the steep grades through the Rocky Mountains. The east–west route was selected by the SpaceX corporation for study for what it calls hyperloop technology.

The Gulf Coast is another corridor through a megaregion that is on the Federal Railroad Administration map as a high-speed rail corridor. So far, the only proposal is to restore twice-a-day Amtrak service between New Orleans and Mobile, Alabama.

In Arizona, a preferred route has been selected for Amtrak to offer train service between Phoenix and Tucson along the I-10 corridor with a possible stop in Tempe. Local activists plan to try to interest Virgin Trains in the route. But there is no mass transit except local buses at the station locations.

Every megaregion is different, but some of them have already made progress toward balancing transportation at the level of the Northeast megaregion. The next chapter is about what should happen next.

CHAPTER 6:

Achieving Balanced Transportation in Megaregions

A regional transportation system does not become balanced until all its parts are operating effectively. Highways, arterial streets, and local streets are essential, and every megaregion has them, although there is often a big backlog of needed repairs, especially for bridges. Airports for long-distance travel are also recognized as essential, and there are major airports in all the evolving megaregions. Both highways and airports are overloaded at peak periods in the megaregions because of gaps in the rest of the transportation system. Predictions for 2040, when the megaregions will be far more developed than they are today, show that there will be much worse traffic congestion and more airport delays.

What is needed to create a better balance? Passenger rail service that is fast enough to be competitive with driving and with some short airplane trips, commuter rail to major employment centers to take some travelers off highways, and improved local transit systems, especially those that make use of exclusive transit rights-of-way, again to reduce the number of cars on highways and arterial roads. Bicycle paths, sidewalks, and pedestrian paths are also important for reducing car trips in neighborhoods and business centers.

Implementing Fast-Enough Passenger Rail

Long-distance Amtrak trains and commuter rail on conventional, unelectrified tracks are powered by diesel locomotives that can attain a maximum permitted speed of 79 miles per hour, which works out to average operating speeds of 30 to 50 miles per hour.[1] At these speeds, trains are not competitive with driving or even short airline flights.

Trains that can attain 110 miles per hour and can operate at average speeds of 70 miles per hour are fast enough to help balance transportation in megaregions. A trip that takes two to three hours by rail can be competitive with a one-hour flight because of the need to allow an hour and a half or more to get to the boarding area through security, plus the time needed to pick up checked baggage. A two-to-three-hour train trip can be competitive with driving when the distance between destinations is more than two hundred miles—particularly for business travelers who want to sit and work on the train. Of course, the trains also have to be frequent enough, and the traveler's destination needs to be easily reachable from a train station.

An important factor in reaching higher railway speeds is the recent federal law requiring all trains to have a positive train control safety system, where automated devices manage train separation to avoid collisions, as well as to prevent excessive speeds and deal with track repairs and other temporary situations. What are called high-speed trains in the United States, averaging 70 miles per hour, need gate controls at grade crossings, upgraded tracks, and trains with tilt technology—as on the Acela trains—to permit faster speeds around curves. The Virgin Trains in Florida have diesel-electric locomotives with an electrical generator on board that drives the train but is powered by a diesel engine. The faster the train needs to operate, the larger, and heavier, these diesel-electric locomotives have to be, setting an effective speed limit on this technology. The faster speeds possible on the portion of Amtrak's Acela service north of New Haven, Connecticut, came after the entire line was electrified, as engines that get their power from lines along the track can be smaller and much lighter, and thus go faster. Catenary or third-rail electric trains, like Amtrak's Acela, can attain speeds of 150 miles per hour, but only a few portions of the tracks now permit this, and average operating speeds are much lower.

Possible Alternatives to Fast-Enough Trains

True electric high-speed rail can attain maximum operating speeds of 150 to 220 miles per hour, with average operating speeds from 120 to 200 miles per hour. These trains need their own grade-separated track structure, which means new alignments, which are expensive to build. In some places the property-acquisition problem may make a new alignment impossible, unless tunnels are used. True high speeds may be attained by the proposed Texas Central train from Dallas to Houston, and on some portions of the California High-Speed Rail line, should it ever be completed. All of the California line is to be electrified, but some sections will be conventional tracks so that average operating speeds will be lower.

Maglev technology is sometimes mentioned as the ultimate solution to attaining high-speed rail travel. A maglev train travels just above a guideway using magnetic levitation and is propelled by electromagnetic energy. There is an operating maglev train connecting the center of Shanghai to its Pudong International Airport. It can reach a top speed of 267 miles per hour, although its average speed is much lower, as the distance is short and most of the trip is spent getting up to speed or decelerating. The Chinese government has not, so far, used this technology in any other application while building a national system of long-distance, high-speed electric trains. However, there has been a recent announcement of a proposed Chinese maglev train that can attain speeds of 375 miles per hour.[2]

The Hyperloop is a proposed technology that would, in theory, permit passenger trains to travel through large tubes from which all air has been evacuated, and would be even faster than today's highest-speed trains. Elon Musk has formed a company to develop this virtually frictionless mode of travel, which would have speeds to make it competitive with medium- and even long-distance airplane travel. However, the Hyperloop technology is not yet ready to be applied to real travel situations, and the infrastructure to support it, whether an elevated system or a tunnel, will have all the problems of building conventional high-speed rail on separate guideways, and will also be even more expensive, as a tube has to be constructed as well as the train.

Megaregions Need Fast-Enough Trains Now

Even if new technology someday creates long-distance passenger trains with travel times competitive with airplanes, passenger traffic will still benefit from upgrading rail service to fast-enough trains for many of the trips within a megaregion, now and in the future. States already have the responsibility of financing passenger trains in megaregion rail corridors. Section 209 of the federal Passenger Rail Investment and Improvement Act of 2008 requires states to pay 85 percent of operating costs for all Amtrak routes of less than 750 miles (the legislation exempts the Northeast Corridor) as well as capital maintenance costs of the Amtrak equipment they use, plus support costs for such programs as safety and marketing. California's Caltrans and Capitol Corridor Joint Powers Authority, Connecticut, Indiana,[3] Illinois, Maine's Northern New England Passenger Rail Authority, Massachusetts, Michigan, Missouri, New York, North Carolina, Oklahoma, Oregon, Pennsylvania, Texas, Vermont, Virginia, Washington, and Wisconsin all have agreements with Amtrak to operate their state corridor services.[4] Amtrak has agreements with the freight railroads that own the tracks, and by law, its operations have priority over freight trains.

At present it appears that upgrading these corridor services to fast-enough trains will also be primarily the responsibility of the states, although they may be able to receive federal grants and loans. The track improvements being financed by the State of Michigan (see chapter 5) are an example of the way a state can take control over rail service. These tracks will eventually be part of 110-mile-per-hour service between Chicago and Detroit, with commitments from not just Michigan but also Illinois and Indiana. Fast-enough service between Chicago and Detroit could become a major organizer in an evolving megaregion, with stops at key cities along the way, including Kalamazoo, Battle Creek, and Ann Arbor.

Cooperation among states for faster train service requires formal agreements, in this case, the Midwest Interstate Passenger Rail Compact. The participants are Illinois, Indiana, Kansas, Michigan, Minnesota, Missouri, Nebraska, North Dakota, Ohio, and Wisconsin. There is also an advocacy organization to support the objectives of the compact, the Midwest Interstate Passenger Rail Commission.

States could, in future, reach operating agreements with a private company such as Virgin Trains USA, but the private company would have to negotiate its own agreement with the freight railroads, and also negotiate its own dispatching priorities. Virgin Trains says in its prospectus that it can finance track improvements itself. If the Virgin Trains service in Florida proves to be profitable, it could lead to other private investments in fast-enough trains.

Connecting Fast-Enough Rail to Airports

Air-traffic delays are a familiar part of travel. Many delays are caused by weather, but some congestion is caused by capacity problems at the airports: not enough gates, or too many planes for the available runways. Takeoffs and landings at the major airports are expected to increase an average of about 1.9 percent a year between now and 2038.[5] Passengers who can choose fast-enough rail over air travel can relieve some of the growth pressures on airports as well as improving the finances for the trains.

The fast-enough train route being studied between Chicago and Detroit passes close enough to Detroit's international airport that a stop could be connected to the airport by an automated people mover. The trip would be similar to the AirTrain JFK connecting the Jamaica railway station—and the New York City transit system—to John F. Kennedy International Airport, a distance of several miles. (See figure 6-1.) The airport serving Kalamazoo and Battle Creek is even closer to the train route. Airport stops do not show up on the map accompanying the feasibility study, but the potential to balance the transportation systems

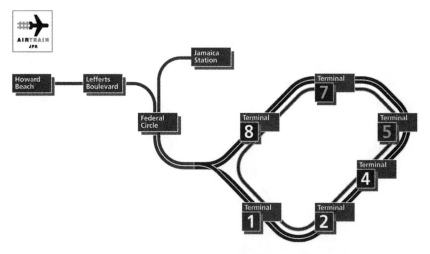

Figure 6-1: The AirTrain links the terminals at John F. Kennedy Airport in New York City as well as connecting to the Long Island Rail Road station in Jamaica, Queens, and to the New York City subway system. Airport–railroad and airport–transit connections are essential for balancing transportation in megaregions.

in the Detroit–Chicago megaregion would be much enhanced if airport connections are included.

Six airlines currently offer nonstop flights in each direction between Kalamazoo–Battle Creek and Detroit. The distance between Detroit and the center of Kalamazoo is around 140 miles; from downtown Battle Creek it is a little less. Driving time is just over two hours. Fast-enough trains should be competitive with driving and with the airline flights, but there would need to be at least seven trains a day in each direction, the number of trains Amtrak currently operates between Milwaukee and Chicago.

A private group, the Midwest High Speed Rail Association, is promoting a link to O'Hare International Airport using the Metra commuter rail tracks, a change that would permit direct access to an airport station for Amtrak trains. The link would modify existing freight rail tracks to permit trains to cross the center of the city and head for the airport. Alternatively, a people mover such as the AirTrain JFK could connect O'Hare to a new Amtrak stop on the line that goes from Chicago's Union Station to Milwaukee. The trains from Detroit also go to Union Station, opening the possibility of travel from cities in Michigan to O'Hare and other destinations between Chicago and Milwaukee by changing trains in Chicago. Comparable opportunities for airport connections can be found in all the megaregions.

Commuter Lines and Transit Systems

Most cities in megaregions have transit agencies and may also have commuter rail lines that extend out beyond the limits of the transit system and are operated by a state department of transportation or other state agency. Transit systems can be traditional heavy rail, light rail, or busways. A large part of all transit systems consist of buses sharing streets with local cars and trucks. These bus routes are indispensable for reaching all points in today's dispersed cities. There is also the possibility of developing bus rapid transit (BRT), which emulates rail transit by operating on an exclusive right-of-way, using defined station locations spaced a half mile or more apart, and boarding passengers all at once with their fares already paid. Chapter 7 discusses introducing BRT along local highways that have become commercial corridors, which could open up locations for more intensive development, including more affordable housing.

Because of the way metropolitan regions, and now megaregions, have been growing, trains and transit do not serve all the potential destinations. Critics acknowledge the usefulness of long-established trains and transit in older cities, but claim it does not make sense to introduce new rail lines to improve and extend the newer systems. They claim that rail and transit will never serve significant percentages of all trips, that financing them is all about nostalgia, and what people want and need is the flexibility of automobile travel.

Figure 1-3 in chapter 1, the map of commuting patterns in the Chicago megaregion by Garrett G. D. Nelson and Alisdair Rae, is one strong refutation of this argument. The map documents existing journeys to work within megaregions—and other, smaller metropolitan areas. The heavy lines on the map, which record large numbers of commuter trips, may mostly be describing trips by car, but they illustrate daily demands along a route that could be supplemented or replaced by a train or transit. But switching from cars to trains or transit requires interconnecting all the components of the transportation system.

Consider the two cities at either end of the proposed Texas Central high-speed line from Dallas to Houston. The backers of this proposal say that taking the trip by train will be at least an hour shorter than driving, and fifty minutes faster than making the short flight by air under the best conditions. However, as noted in chapter 5, passengers arriving at the high-speed terminal in Houston will find themselves seven miles from the nearest Houston METRORail transit station. Until there is a connection, passengers will be dependent on taxis and car services, and the time saved by taking the train is likely to be lost in getting to the part of Houston that is the actual end of the trip.

Passengers arriving at Houston's George Bush Intercontinental Airport have a similar problem: no good transit connections; and Houston's transit system has yet to be extended to the city's William P. Hobby Airport. These arriving or departing passengers need to rent a car, rely on a taxi or a car service, or take an airport bus. If the transit system connected to the major points of arrival and departure, many passengers could go to or from many other places in Houston, avoiding congested highways and the expense and nuisance of renting a car or waiting for a ride to arrive.

At Dallas, again as noted in chapter 5, the high-speed rail terminal will be located within people mover–connection distance of the convention center and its adjacent Dallas Area Rapid Transit (DART) station. Passengers arriving at Dallas–Fort Worth International Airport today can use the airport DART station located at Terminal A. The connection at the other Dallas airport is not so direct, requiring a shuttle bus with fifteen-minute head times to go between the Inwood/Love Field Station and the Love Field terminal. But, according to the DART website, the Green and Orange Lines at this station provide direct service to and from "the Dallas/Fort Worth International Airport, Irving, Carrollton, Farmers Branch, northeastern Dallas, Downtown Dallas and the Fair Park area. Passengers can transfer to the Red Line or Blue Line in Downtown Dallas to connect to Richardson, Plano, Garland, Rowlett and southern Dallas. Those traveling west toward Fort Worth can transfer to the Trinity Railway Express at Victory Station."[6]

Houston needs to have the same kinds of interconnections available in Dallas if the new train connection is going to be effective.

Highways in Megaregions

As highways become increasingly congested for longer periods, what seems to be the obvious cure is to widen the highways to add more lanes, despite substantial evidence that adding lanes soon induces more traffic and congestion soon returns, as exemplified by congestion on the Katy Freeway in Houston, parts of which have twenty-six lanes.[7] Funds for highway improvements, and also for transit, go through metropolitan planning organizations (MPOs), which date from the Federal-Aid Highway Act of 1962. The boards of these organizations represent the governmental bodies within their boundaries, and they and their staffs are supposed to ensure that the available highway and transit funds are spent effectively. MPOs vary in size and are called by different names, depending on the size, and the history, of the metropolitan area.

The Delaware Valley Regional Planning Commission is an MPO that covers five counties in Pennsylvania and four in New Jersey, but most MPOs are contained within individual states and are closely associated with each state's Department of Transportation. When MPOs were first created, thinking in terms of regions was a big step forward from considering transportation needs only for cities and towns. At the time, megaregions were a subject of discussion only among urban geographers. Having MPOs adapt to the reality of their place within a larger megaregion is difficult. Determining which projects get what funds is a complex political issue, and the MPOs have enough problems establishing their own priorities that they haven't given comparable attention to their place in a larger megaregion. Geographic information systems (GIS) mapping of conservation priorities and the ability to compare these maps with GIS projections of future development will give MPOs powerful tools for making decisions in a regional context. In Florida, where the entire state is close to being a megaregion, there are already alliances among some MPOs. In California there is a statewide organization that includes all eighteen MPOs within the state. Right now it is essentially a support organization, but it could be a forum for discussing environmental and development issues that involve the two megaregions within the state. In general, it will be easier for MPOs to establish interagency committees to deal with specific multiregional issues, rather than seeking to create a new planning structure for an entire megaregion.

There are two big questions about allocating future highway funds within megaregions. One is whether a strategy of allocating more funds to transit or train connections could take some of the growth pressures off highways, reducing the number of new lanes that need to be constructed. The second is how to configure wider highways.

A ten- or sixteen-lane highway could need a different design beyond adding more lanes. Some of the lanes could be allocated to high-occupancy vehicles (HOVs), a lane in each direction could be reserved for buses, other lanes could be reserved for through traffic. Local passenger and freight traffic could be channeled to lanes on the far sides of the highway, and might have more frequent access points. Figure 6-2 shows a typical highway expansion using HOV lanes in the center, lanes that can also be used by buses. The most striking thing about this photograph is how wide highways have become, and how they divide the areas they go through. Some highways these days can have more than five lanes in each direction, plus HOV lanes and even service roads.

As shown by the Katy Freeway example, induced traffic raises the question of whether it might often be more cost effective to divert some passenger trips to trains or BRT services rather than continuing to pay for adding lanes to highways. Where the potential widened highway extends through areas covered by more than one MPO, it makes sense for the organizations to agree about configurations, or about a strategy to reduce the required widening by investing in trains or transit.

Figure 6-2: Reversible HOV (high-occupancy vehicle) lanes, shown here on I-395 in Alexandria, Virginia, are a way of reducing congestion at peak periods. Widening highways by adding more lanes is always difficult, and has become impossible in many places because of development along the route.

Walking and Cycling

Providing bicycle paths and sidewalks is a local issue; their significance for a megaregion is to make trains and transit more effective. Having compact, walkable neighborhoods and business centers makes it possible for people to walk from a transit station, or from a parking garage, to many different destinations within a quarter of a mile to half a mile. Requiring sidewalks as part of each street design would appear to be axiomatic, but sidewalks are often omitted not only on newer suburban highways but also in local subdivisions. Sidewalk standards and requirements need to be in every subdivision ordinance, and also should be part of street-design policies for every local government.

Making bicycles a more important part of transportation has strong support from many people, but bicycles are not as easy to accommodate as pedestrians. If bicycles are used for commuting, there needs to be bicycle storage and changing facilities at the work destination. Trains and multicar transit can be adapted to make it possible to bring bicycles

Figure 6-3: According to the New York City Department of Transportation, eliminating one traffic lane (and narrowing the lanes) on Ninth Avenue in Midtown Manhattan, and then adding a protected bicycle lane, as shown, has reduced the number of crashes with injuries by almost half, and encouraged an increase of 65 percent in the number of bicycle riders using the route.

on board, so cyclists can travel longer distances. The entrances for bicycles need to be clearly marked on the exterior of the train or transit car, and fare collection has to permit people to board at multiple entrances. Bicycles can move much faster than pedestrians, and if a cyclist going full speed hits a pedestrian, the results of the collision can be serious.

Jan Gehl, a Danish architect who has spent much of his professional life making cities more hospitable to people traveling on foot, once said to me, "Bicycles are not people, or perhaps they are only half people."[8] Gehl is very much in favor of providing bicycle lanes in cities, but they need to be protected from cars, and pedestrians need to be protected from bicycles. The photo of a bicycle lane on Ninth Avenue in New York City (figure 6-3) shows changes made to create a protected bicycle path. The street loses one lane of traffic, but there are big gains in safety and bicycle use. Standards for bicycle paths should be added to the street-design handbooks for public works departments in cities, and to the subdivision ordinance where new development is taking place.

CHAPTER 7:

Inequities Built into Megaregions

Megaregions are developing in very unequal ways. Historic downtowns within a megaregion may be thriving, and neighborhoods near these centers can be preferred places to live, but there are also high-crime, very low-income areas nearby. Some suburbs are made up of estates and country-club neighborhoods, others have grown up as new middle-income housing tracts, but there are also older suburbs with deteriorating housing and many vacant stores. Some cities within the megaregion may have been bypassed, their original economic base gone. A high proportion of new investment is going to the edges of the cities that make up the emerging megaregions, where almost all people live in market-rate housing, commute to work by car, and seldom go into older urban areas.

The expected population growth in megaregions can be an opportunity to reduce serious inequality issues affecting where people live, access to schools and services, and journeys to work. Projected growth is also an opportunity to create alternative locations for people who live in areas at risk from climate change, often the people who currently have the fewest choices. Correcting inequities is a significant factor in the need for designing megaregions, because if most growth continues at the suburban fringes, isolation of less-favored areas will become worse, and journeys to work will become increasingly difficult.

Inequality has been a driving force for urban growth ever since cities stopped being surrounded by walls. People with higher incomes can choose what they think are the best places to live. In North American cities, the separation of the rich from the less fortunate usually began in the nineteenth century with a street of mansions leading away from the center, often up a hill or upwind of manufacturing districts. The initial direction of fashionable growth continued as streetcars and railroads enabled cities to expand, with the rich moving on from initially fashionable areas, which may have been overrun by other urban uses, to exclusive suburbs farther out, generally on the same side of the city. Later, when highways enabled the dispersal of suburbs and the decentralization of jobs and housing, new urban centers grew up on the side of the city already established as the preferred location. These real estate distinctions tend to fade out beyond the first highway ring road, where access becomes more even and places are farther and farther away from the least affluent parts of the region. Exceptions are where urban growth has enfolded older, smaller cities with their own growth patterns and real estate distinctions.

Highways were also used to restructure older areas in ways that favored investors and downtown businesses. The process of acquiring rights-of-way dispersed poor people from urban neighborhoods viewed as a blighting influence on nearby property, and highways built barriers between downtown and inner-city neighborhoods.

Inequality Visible from Space

Figure 7-1 is a Google satellite image of Bridgeport, Connecticut, part of the New York City metropolitan region, which in turn is part of the East Coast megaregion. Bridgeport is the governmental center of

Figure 7-1: The inequality between affluent suburban Fairfield, Connecticut, on the left, with its country clubs, wooded open spaces, and larger residential lots, and the distressed city of Bridgeport at right is clearly visible from space in this Google view.

Fairfield County, one of the country's most prosperous areas, but the city has lost most of its manufacturing base, and its corporate headquarters have mostly migrated to Bridgeport suburbs.

The downtown is located within the L-shape formed by highway barriers on the right of the photo. The dominant growth vector is to the west, on the left of this image, where you can see the affluent neighborhood around the Brooklawn Country Club's golf course in the neighboring suburb of Fairfield. The boundary between Fairfield and Bridgeport shows up distinctly, as Fairfield has larger lot zoning with more space for lawns and trees.

Large open areas around Bridgeport's downtown are remnants of old factories and of residential areas where many of the houses have become vacant and been torn down. Twenty-two percent of the people in the entire city of Bridgeport live below the poverty line, meaning that there are neighborhoods where the percentage living in poverty is much higher. Despite redevelopment efforts, there is little growth in jobs or housing, and overall property values are declining. An article in *The Atlantic* a few years ago described Bridgeport as the "epicenter of American inequality."[2]

The Legacy of Redlining and Racially Restrictive Covenants

The difference in development beyond the west side of the Bridgeport city boundary—so striking it can be seen in satellite views—is partly the result of Fairfield's larger-lot zoning, which raises house prices. Another important cause has been federal government policies beginning in 1933 that magnified and institutionalized real estate trends. The pioneering account of "redlining" and other government actions that contribute to geographic inequality can be found in Kenneth Jackson's *Crabgrass Frontier: The Suburbanization of the United States.*[3] The Home Owners' Loan Corporation, an early New Deal program, provided federal guarantees for mortgages with relatively small amounts of money down, and monthly payments that would completely pay off the mortgage after what was then considered a long term, such as twenty years. This economic-revitalization program was especially useful because it did not require direct expenditures by the federal government.

As Jackson has documented, the officials administering the program were concerned about the repayment of the loans their agency would guarantee. They established and mapped four grades of mortgage safety, drawn from then current real estate practice: Sought-after, growing neighborhoods were designated A and mapped in green. Older neighborhoods that were "still desirable" were given a grade of B and mapped in blue. C (yellow) described neighborhoods thought of as declining, and D neighborhoods, coded red, indicated places where decline was considered complete.

The analogy to traffic signals is clear. Loans should not be made in the red districts. The agency maintained secret "residential security" maps in local offices to guide loan approvals. Any neighborhood with African American residents was mapped as red. The presence of Jews in affluent, growing neighborhoods demoted these places from green to blue. Concentrations of recent immigrants tended to have a C rating, putting a caution-inducing yellow tone over maps of where they lived.

These policies responded to a real estate market where racially restrictive covenants were a widespread part of residential deeds. A typical covenant specified that "no part of said property or any portion thereof shall be . . . occupied by any person not of the Caucasian race."[4] These covenants were legally enforceable until the Supreme Court declared them unconstitutional in 1948. However, that decision permitted private parties, such as seller and buyer, to continue to observe them until the federal Fair Housing Act of 1968 finally made such covenants illegal.

The Federal Housing Administration (FHA), which replaced and enlarged the responsibilities of the Home Owners' Loan Corporation in 1934, inherited the "residential security" policies and maps. After World War II, an additional mortgage guarantee program, the VA home loan, was made available to war veterans through the Veterans Administration. The color codes continued to guide federal government mortgage loan guarantees during the post–World War II period, when many of today's suburbs, such as Fairfield, Connecticut, grew into their present-day form. Mortgage-backed securities from three other federal housing programs—the Federal National Mortgage Association, the Federal Home Loan Mortgage Corporation, and the Government National Mortgage Association—made housing investment available nationally.

Kenneth Jackson concluded that an important side effect of creating these agencies was the way they channeled investment away from older areas. Investors from places like Bridgeport could buy securities backed by mortgages in other, faster-growing areas rather than in their local economy.[5]

A more comprehensive and more recent account of government complicity in racial discrimination is *The Color of Law: A Forgotten History of How Our Government Segregated America* by Richard Rothstein, which documents governmental actions in addition to redlining, including segregating public housing and the New Deal new towns, enabling discrimination in the work force, preventing racial integration in neighborhoods, keeping schools in cities underfunded, and generally allowing many private discriminatory actions to go unchallenged. Rothstein's central argument is that, as government was complicit in enabling racial discrimination, it continues to have an obligation to take actions to correct it.[6]

While the FHA backed some mortgages for apartments, most of the federal guarantees went for individual houses. For many urban apartment dwellers after World War II, the mortgage payments for a whole house on a private lot could be less than what they were paying to rent in the city. Local zoning policies reflected this demand. Residential suburbs grew up that were almost entirely composed of single-family houses, as were the local school districts.

Up until at least the passage of the Fair Housing Act in 1968, it was still routine for developers and real estate agents to exclude African Americans from buying or renting a house. Following typical zoning codes, most of these suburbs were further segregated by mapping large lots in one location, smaller lots in another. These zoning policies enforced economic segregation, as smaller lots—except in a few urban centers—meant smaller, less expensive houses.

As most school districts are funded by local property taxes, an economic disincentive against apartments was built into most suburbs. Apartments for people aged fifty-five and older are usually not considered a problem, as the tenants would probably not include children, but an apartment complex for ordinary families is unlikely to return as much revenue per student to the school district as a subdivision of houses.

In more rural areas, zoning lots could be kept large enough—typically two acres or more—that the houses could depend on wells and septic tanks on each property. This zoning practice created a disincentive for smaller lot sizes or any kind of apartment, which would require installation of piped water supplies and sewer systems paid for by all property owners in the community.

Concentrated Poverty: Neighborhoods where 40 percent of the residents, or more, have incomes below the poverty level meet the US Census definition of extreme poverty. These places are part of the legacy of redlining and racially restrictive covenants. The impact on people living in such neighborhoods was vividly described by William Julius Wilson in *The Truly Disadvantaged: The Inner City, the Underclass, and Public Policy*, originally published in 1987, where he used terms such as *concentration of poverty, concentrated poverty*, and *the concentration effect* in describing how living in these places made the problems of poverty even worse. A high proportion of the people living in concentrated poverty were—and are—African American. In an afterword to the second edition, published in 2012, Wilson summarized subsequent research by others, concluding that—while there had been some improvement in the 1990s—concentrated poverty has persisted, and is increasing again.[7]

Peter Dreier, John Mollenkopf, and Todd Swanstrom, in the 2014 edition of their book *Place Matters: Metropolitics for the Twenty-First Century*, describe neighborhoods of concentrated poverty as more dangerous, and consequently more stressful for inhabitants, because of high crime rates. People living in these neighborhoods have high unemployment, fewer social ties, more incidence of serious illness, and lower life expectancies. City schools and other public services are deficient. These neighborhoods are also highly segregated; many continue to consist of predominantly black residents.[8]

Gentrification: Gentrification describes a situation where people with more resources move into a lower-income community, raising property values and displacing the previous residents. The term, which has overtones of irony and understatement, was first used in print by British sociologist Ruth Glass in an introduction to a book of essays by various authors published in 1964.[9]

The recent development boom in some formerly redlined or yellow-lined urban neighborhoods is double-edged. It is good for the city's economies, and good for property owners, but not for low-income tenants concentrated in these places by earlier government policies. Longtime residents can be priced out of whole neighborhoods, and the affordable alternative can be much less desirable areas, also with high concentrations of poverty. The problem with gentrification is thus not the reinvestment in older areas, but the lack of alternatives for the residents who have to move.

There used to be high percentages of city residents living in slum conditions that did not meet even the basic requirements of the building code. Decades of slum clearance, new housing construction, and the abandonment of the worst housing have improved the quality of what is available, but has also led to housing shortages and a crisis of affordability. Matthew Desmond's *Evicted: Poverty and Profit in the American City* tells, through accounts of what happens to eight families in Milwaukee trying to find a place where they can afford to live, how unfair and exploitive the current housing situation is for those with the fewest resources.[10] And while the gentrification trend receives a lot of attention as a sign of urban revival, and for the accompanying problems of displacement, it does not affect many older urban neighborhoods, where conditions are actually getting worse.[11]

Housing Affordability Is Driving Urban Sprawl

Where can newcomers to a city, or recent graduates, or new families find an affordable place to live? For many, established residential areas and suburbs have become too expensive, and finding affordable housing can mean traveling long distances.

Figure 7-2 shows the Southern California megaregion at night from space in 2014. Unlike the East Coast megaregion, which grew up around a series of historic downtowns, Southern California has only two main economic centers: the Los Angeles region, on the Pacific Coast in the center of the photo, and San Diego–Tijuana at the right, farther along the coastline. Much of the development shown radiating out from Los Angeles, and skipping over intermediate mountain ranges, has been driven by a search for more affordable housing. The median house price, as sold, in Los Angeles in 2019 was close to $700,000, according to Zillow, and the median rent was $3,500 a month. To find a suburban median house price of around $300,000 could mean commuting from

Figure 7-2: The growth of the Southern California megaregion has been intensified by the search for affordable housing. Los Angeles is at the center of this NASA photo, with the San Diego–Tijuana region at the right. Growth from Los Angeles has skipped over intervening mountain ranges to suburbs more than sixty miles away.

Lancaster or Palmdale in the Antelope Valley, more than sixty miles from Los Angeles—and that is still not affordable for many. Apartment rentals in Lancaster start around $1,200 a month for a one-bedroom.

The permanent zoning and infrastructure of many established urban residential neighborhoods and most suburban communities favor single-family houses. And moving to these places has become less affordable than it used to be. The thousands of houses mass-produced in Levittown, Long Island, are an often-cited example of the kind of development supported by FHA mortgages after World War II. The lowest-priced Levittown houses currently available—those that remain close to the original configuration of three bedrooms, one bath, and a carport—are listed at $185,000. That house would originally have cost about $8,000, including a quarter-acre lot, about $84,000 today according to the US Bureau of Labor Statistics consumer price index. The cost of admission to a suburban lifestyle has more than doubled in Levittown, and is higher in many places. According to the Federal Reserve Bank of Saint Louis, the median price of a single-family house in the United States was $330,000 in the third quarter of 2018.[12]

Attempts to open up urban residential neighborhoods and suburbs to more affordable row houses and apartments through lawsuits and state legislation have not yet had much success. The best-known example is probably the sequence of lawsuits leading to court decisions requiring affordable housing in Mount Laurel, New Jersey, followed by the passage of New Jersey's Fair Housing Act in 1985. The act required that each New Jersey community accept its fair share of affordable housing, as determined by a Council on Affordable Housing.

How this works out in practice was described in an article in the *New York Times* about Harding Township, New Jersey, a community mostly zoned for houses on three acres or more, with lots served by private wells and septic tanks. The township's original quota for permitting affordable housing under New Jersey's Fair Housing Act was 350 units. That number was eventually negotiated down to 176 units, 40 of which will be age-restricted. Most of the units will be built near Route 202, a commercial corridor at the southwestern corner of the township, where the zoning permits eight houses to the acre.[13] In some situations, New Jersey communities can also buy their way out of accommodating Fair Housing Act requirements by contributing to affordable housing in other jurisdictions.

Massachusetts has a law that permits local zoning adjustment boards to grant onetime permits that override zoning restrictions for affordable housing. But, looking at the whole United States, Fair Housing quotas and hard-won exceptions to restrictive regulations have resulted in only minor amounts of affordable housing. The bias toward single-family houses, created by government programs but now taken for granted by residents, has proved difficult to overcome.[14] And none of this "affordable" housing is within the means of the people trying to find a place to live whom Matthew Desmond describes in *Evicted.* The United States continues to be a deeply unequal place.

Market Forces Can Make Some Housing More Affordable

There are some growth management initiatives that can help open up older suburbs to more affordable housing and take some of the development pressures off the urban fringe. Figure 7-3 shows the central part of the East Coast megaregion at night. Philadelphia is on the left at the bottom of the photograph, the New York City metropolitan area is in the middle, and Hartford, Connecticut, is on the upper right.

If you look along the Connecticut shore to the right of the intense lights of the New York region, there are four bright spots representing the centers of Stamford, Norwalk, Bridgeport, and New Haven. The leafy suburbs around them show up as much darker areas. The glowing line connecting these cities is Route 1, which, under various names, is the traditional main street of the communities along this part of the Connecticut shore. Route 1 is what planners call a *commercial strip*: a relatively narrow band zoned for retail, and possibly office and motels, on both sides of an important local highway route. This zoning pattern has created commercial strips within residential areas almost everywhere in the United States.

As the retail market changes because of e-commerce, commercial strips, with their high ratio of parking lots to buildings, are becoming land banks. Along with the vacant land in passed-over urban areas

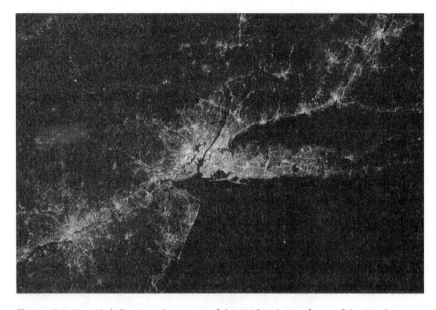

Figure 7-3: New York City is at the center of this NASA photo of part of the Northeast megaregion. The chain of lights heading northeast along the north side of Long Island Sound belongs to Stamford, Norwalk, Bridgeport, and New Haven. The bright line connecting them is Route 1, a commercial corridor that runs through these cities and through the leafy suburbs surrounding them, which show up as dark places in this view. The commercial corridor is becoming a land bank because of the revolution going on in retail. Building apartments and town houses along Route 1 to replace vacant retail structures could open up these cities and suburbs to more affordable housing.

like inner-city Bridgeport, obsolete commercial properties can become a means for diminishing some of the separation between seriously disadvantaged people and everyone else. It should also be possible to increase density in existing "built-out" residential suburbs by permitting accessory housing units on single-family plots, and permitting infill garden apartments and town houses in carefully selected areas. These changes, in turn, will take some of the growth pressures off the outer edges of the urban areas that make up a megaregion, helping to make all development more compact and sustainable. The way to implement such policies is the subject of the next chapter.

CHAPTER 8:

Reducing Inequality in Megaregions

The *Fourth Regional Plan for the New York–New Jersey–Connecticut Metropolitan Area*, published in 2017 by the private, nonprofit Regional Plan Association (RPA), summarized its goal for equity in the region by 2040 with this statement: "The tri-state region should sharply reduce poverty, end homelessness, close gaps in health and wealth that exist along racial, ethnic, and gender lines, and become one of the least segregated regions in the nation instead of one of the most segregated."

The RPA supports this goal with twenty-four policies. Five policies relate to affordable housing, three require more inclusive decision-making, five are concerned with access to economic opportunity, six with protection from environmental pollution and the effects of climate change, and five with transportation improvements.[1]

Many of these policies depend on local governments for implementation, but there are possible planning and design innovations throughout megaregions that can make it easier for people to find affordable homes closer to where they work, and also gain access to suburban school systems. Opening up more areas to town houses and apartments also creates more opportunities to create subsidized housing outside older urban centers, helping to mitigate concentrated poverty, which research shows makes every kind of social problem worse. Equity is also closely related to transportation, and to managing development within its natural context. A balanced transportation system will improve access to jobs, and better environmental management can help the people who are most at risk from climate change.

Commercial Corridors as a Road to More Equality

Driving along a highway lined with small retail buildings and big parking lots is so familiar that people don't realize it is entirely created by zoning regulations. The real estate market has adjusted to generally accepted zoning practice, which defines narrow districts of concentrated retail uses along local highways. Sometimes small offices and motels are also permitted, but usually not places to live. Instead, residential neighborhoods are mapped to come right up to these strips of commercial development on both sides of the highway.

Figure 8-1 is a Google Earth view of the Clarkson Road intersection along the Manchester Road in Ellisville, Missouri, a suburb of Saint Louis. The satellite photograph shows almost every frontage occupied by strip shopping centers or commercial buildings, with parking lots using up most of the land. Until recently, property values were too high for residential buildings. Now, however, e-commerce is pulling tenants out of commercial corridors. You can see evidence of this change in the photograph. In the foreground on the left, you can see a cluster of parking lots where the building has been scraped to make way for some future use. In the shopping center across the highway, the Kmart store that anchored it is closed, and many of the other spaces are vacant. The surviving tenants include small restaurants, a nail parlor, and a tanning salon—which all require people to come into the store.[2]

Figure 8-1: Vacant buildings and empty parking lots along the Manchester Road, in suburban Ellisville, Missouri, show that this typical commercial corridor is becoming a land bank, because of the changes e-commerce is making to retail. These properties are no longer too valuable to be used for apartments and town houses. Redevelopment could add housing options adjacent to nearby residential neighborhoods and take some of the growth pressures off areas at the edge of the metropolitan region.

Commercial corridors, with their vacant buildings and large parking lots, are becoming great opportunities. Of course, there will always be some services you can't buy on the internet. In addition to the kinds of tenants still in the Kmart shopping center, there could be a health club, a drop-off location for packages, or a dry cleaner—all to be found around the same intersection in Ellisville. But a substantial part of this district is becoming obsolete: the parking lots are nowhere near full, and buildings are vacant or underused.

There is also growing demand for residential buildings that are more affordable, and less expensive to maintain, than the traditional, single-family suburban house. At the edges of the photograph, you can see that more affordable types of market-rate housing are already permitted in Ellisville next to its commercial corridor. Town houses are visible in the lower left, and garden apartments at the top of the photo on the right. But much of the demand for this kind of housing is being met on the urbanizing edges of the emerging megaregions, where you can see town houses and apartment complexes—once found only in urban and suburban centers—being built right at the edge of farms and woodland.

Row houses and multifamily housing could be the way to open out-dated commercial corridors to new development while reducing growth pressures at the rural fringe. Fewer people would have to drive long distances to get to their jobs. As property values in these corridors are no longer too high for residential buildings, zoning is the major remaining problem: it usually does not permit residences in these kinds of commercial zones. Zoning regulations can be revised to permit a mix of uses that includes apartments and town houses, and adopted corridor master plans can shape the new development into walkable, mixed-use places.

What about parking? The commercial uses that continue to be viable in these locations are generally small, and don't need the large parking lots left over from the previous generation of development. Parking for town houses can be in a garage within each home. Parking for garden apartments is often accommodated in a single-story garage half a level belowground, underneath the buildings. Figure 8-2, a drawing by Freedman, Tung + Sasaki Urban Design, shows how apartments and row houses could replace obsolete retail development in parts of a commercial corridor (in this example, along Whittier Boulevard in Montebello, California). The apartments surround courtyards, built over parking, and the streets of town houses are constructed closer to the existing residential district, where they are in scale with neighboring homes.

Having apartments and town houses next to single-family residential districts opens up opportunities for retired people to downsize to an apartment in the same neighborhood, and for young families to live in apartments or row houses close to the homes where they grew up. While new construction costs much the same wherever it is located,

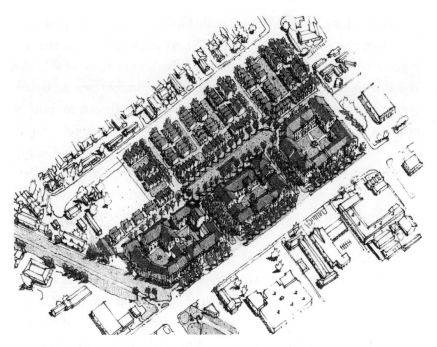

Figure 8-2: This drawing by the firm of Friedman, Tung + Sasaki Urban Design shows how apartments and town houses can be introduced into a commercial corridor, in this example, along Whittier Boulevard in Montebello, California. The apartments surround courtyards built over one level of parking, and the streets of town houses are constructed closer to the existing residential district, where they are in scale with neighboring homes.

row houses and apartments can be more affordable because each unit takes up less land, apartments are usually smaller than houses, and there can be construction cost-savings from building many units at one time. Adding lower-cost options to the housing market makes it easier for schoolteachers, police officers, firefighters, and other not-so-well-paid workers to live in the community where they work. Urban designer Daniel Parolek calls this type of housing the "missing middle" between single-family homes and apartment towers, and areas zoned as commercial corridors are a good location for such buildings.

Having alternatives to single-family houses has obvious benefits for any community. But many people still can't afford only somewhat less expensive row houses and apartments. A portion of these new houses and apartments can be set aside for subsidized housing, creating opportunities for people in disadvantaged urban neighborhoods to move to places with better schools and more access to jobs. A good example for how to go about doing this can be seen in Montgomery County, Maryland, which has, since 1973, managed a program that rewards developers with additional density if they set aside units for affordable and subsidized town houses and apartments. The program applies to all of Montgomery County, which, over time, has resulted in thousands of affordable units. Up-zoned commercial corridors in communities throughout a megaregion, with more affordable housing and bonuses for adding subsidized units, could help people find affordable homes without having to commute long distances from the edge of the city, and some people could move into subsidized row houses and apartments outside distressed inner-city neighborhoods.

The design and development concept for the houses and apartments shown in figure 8-2 could be feasible in the current real estate market. The necessary zoning changes could be adopted in any community that has outmoded commercial-strip zoning, and if a portion of the new housing were not just more affordable but also subsidized, there could be a real reduction in problems of spatial inequality. But are such changes politically feasible?

Political Feasibility of Transforming Commercial Corridors

Decades of redlining and other official programs that actively promoted single-family residences have left local governments with built-in obstacles to adding apartments and row houses. As mentioned in chapter 7, local communities and school districts depend on their property taxes for much of their revenue. Apartments don't return as much property tax per potential student as most individual houses, but a vacant shopping center doesn't support much property tax either. Moving from vacant and underused stores to multifamily housing can and should be managed to restore and maintain tax revenue.

Rezoning plans should combine apartments with other land uses to balance them: retail spaces for stores that continue to be viable, assisted-living developments that benefit from being in a mixed-use walkable area, office space and motels. And, of course, age-restricted housing and luxury condominiums are also useful for supporting school taxes, but should not be the only way to transform outmoded retail districts. State-funded programs for equalizing resources for schools will also be important; making local governments less dependent on property taxes will be critical in making regions more equitable.

Programs to Reuse Areas of Vacant Land in Older Cities

The big areas of vacant land in cities such as Bridgeport, Connecticut (see figure 7-1 in the previous chapter), ought to be able to attract the real estate market back to these bypassed areas. Parts of cities that have become largely vacant still have their streets and utilities, which can make new development there less expensive and easier than it would be at the fast-growing urban fringe, where developers must pay to put in the necessary streets and infrastructure. Making use of vacant, already urbanized land is not happening today at anything like the scale that should be possible. Vacant urban land is usually divided into small parcels with many different owners, and there could be problems from underground fuel tanks and buried debris from demolishing the buildings that used to be there. Big developers will not be attracted until these obstacles are overcome.

What is needed is a government agency with the funding and powers necessary to condemn vacant land and buildings, acquire and consolidate these properties, clear their titles, make sure the zoning is appropriate, and remove any pollutants or other obstacles to new construction. New York State's Empire State Development Corporation could be a prototype for the kind of agency needed to make these interventions in big and small cities within a megaregion. Tracts of this newly assembled land could then be sold to developers along with requirements for how the land should be developed.

Most cities have urban renewal agencies with these powers—often not used wisely in the past, but only big cities are likely to have access to anything like the necessary capital. Most cities do have a large portfolio of land resources, including properties acquired through tax foreclosures, and can create land banks to acquire and hold land until funds for turning these properties into development opportunities can be found. Some big cities, like Detroit, Cleveland, and the Twin Cities, already have such programs.

But cities have seldom been able to create development opportunities by assembling small parcels of vacant land at a scale that would attract major investors, such as the national home-building companies, although there has been success attracting big private developers to former airport sites—Stapleton in Denver and Mueller Municipal in Austin, for example. If the sites are there at the scale of whole new neighborhoods, as at these airports, developers will find the opportunity attractive, and buyers and renters will know they will be part of a coherent community, not just dropped into the existing urban situation. The amount of capital needed to launch an effective program of land assemblage is large, but the state or city agencies should be able to get their investment back when they sell the land to developers, creating a revolving fund that can be used to transform additional parts of cities.

The political problem with bringing relatively affluent buyers and tenants into abandoned parts of central cities is the mirror image of the political problems with introducing people who used to live in other places into rezoned suburban corridors. Even when the urban land is vacant and there is little or no need to relocate anyone to create a new development, the neighbors in the central city are going to ask what value this investment is going to have for them, and whether change means they will soon be priced out of their homes.

One answer has to be that a portion of the new development should be set aside for subsidized housing, as in New York City's Inclusionary Housing Program, established in 1987, which gives developers the opportunity in designated areas for a floor-area bonus in exchange for building units that have permanent rent limits. There is also mandatory inclusionary housing for all residential units in developments above a designated size, again in areas that are predetermined and mapped by the city.[3]

New development in vacant parts of older urban areas should also be accompanied by neighborhood-conservation loan and grant programs to upgrade the housing of people already living in the surrounding blocks. Cities have had neighborhood conservation districts since the 1960s, but they are difficult to administer and are chronically underfunded. But if large-scale private-sector investment in bypassed parts of older cities is to be successful, it has to be supported by conservation of the surrounding areas, and these programs need to begin at the same time as the new construction. In addition, cities should make sure that there are good school buildings, branch libraries, parks, and community centers in these areas. The prospective residents paying market rates for housing will demand them, and the existing neighbors should see these improvements as a benefit of accepting change.

Making such development happen is going to take a carefully managed process of community participation to give the people already living in the area an understanding of the benefits of the proposed development, including awareness that some of the market for the new housing will be former friends and neighbors who would like the opportunity to come back to their churches and familiar connections to the rest of the city, if they can have better living conditions. There is also the potential value from an improved tax base that can help support better schools and services.

Community participation has become an axiomatic part of planning, but special efforts have to be made to manage participation in neighborhoods where many people are too busy trying to survive to attend community meetings. There has to be outreach to local leadership and to institutions, such as churches, that are committed to the neighborhood. The process also has to include city government officials and elected representatives as well as representatives of the investors and developers. A serious problem with community participation in lower-income neighborhoods is a succession of broken promises going back to the Model Cities Program fifty years ago. Is it going to be different this time? Personal commitments are needed from people representing both the private and the public sectors. Local politicians are not necessarily going to be pleased at the prospect of large numbers of new constituents being introduced into their districts, another reason why a community participation process is needed so that the politician's current constituents end up being in favor of the change. If there is strong local opposition, the developers are not going to invest.

Creating attractive new development in places that have been considered unbuildable could have a powerful positive influence on adjoining older neighborhoods. Development of the entire megaregion could become more balanced by diverting some development from the suburban fringe into opportunities created in older cities.

Urban Infill

Another kind of opportunity in existing cities and older suburbs comes from the vacant lots and derelict structures that inevitably occur in well-established neighborhoods. These sites can be used to increase the number of houses and apartments and add a variety of housing types. The risk is that the new development will be out of scale with the existing area, will introduce inappropriate designs, or will become so widespread that the neighborhood is completely changed.

Toronto has created an exemplary program to manage urban infill by writing architectural standards for site plans and buildings to permit a variety of possible housing types at an added density but preserve the scale and appearance of the neighborhood. Figure 8-3 is an illustration from the City of Toronto *Townhouse and Low-Rise Apartment Guidelines*

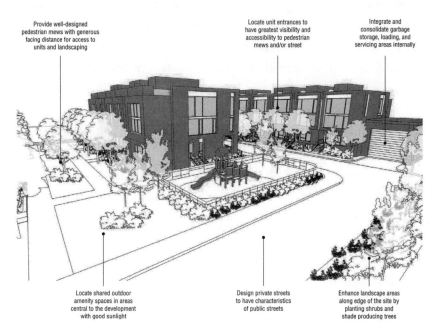

Figure 8-3: Up-zoning of established low-density neighborhoods is being considered in many places. The City of Toronto permits higher-density new development on vacant or underused lots in older neighborhoods, but each plan must be approved individually and conform to the design concepts published in the city's *Townhouse and Low-Rise Apartment Guidelines*. This drawing, from the guidelines, shows an approved way to introduce row houses, stacked row houses, or back-to-back row houses on a small parcel of vacant land in a neighborhood of larger, older homes on individual lots.

showing how a group of row houses, stacked row houses, or back-to-back row houses should be built on a small parcel of vacant land in a neighborhood of larger, older homes on individual lots.[4] With careful design review of these kinds of opportunities, residents in a variety of smaller, more affordable homes can be added to established neighborhoods, while preserving local character and property values.

Letting More People Live in Single-Family Zones

Cities and states have recently started looking at changing single-family zoning to permit more dwelling units in these restrictive zones. Minneapolis has recently approved a plan to permit up to three dwelling units in districts currently zoned only for single-family houses, and Oregon has passed a law that requires larger communities in the state to end single-family restrictions by permitting up to four dwelling units per lot. If the result is that many old houses are torn down, and new duplex and triplex units replace them, then it is going to be important to regulate how these changes take place, the way this kind of management takes place in Toronto. Any city that rezones single-family districts also needs to regulate how the parking is to be provided. If most of the remaining space on a property is paved for parking, the result will not be good design, and it will intensify heat waves and accelerate stormwater runoff. We come back to the design and technical issues raised by these policies in chapter 10.

Seattle is considering a less sweeping set of changes for single-family zones, which could reduce the minimum lot size in some areas and permit the expansion of zones where multiple dwellings are already permitted. Many cities, including Seattle, have already adopted a much less controversial set of provisions that allow the construction of what, in zoning speak, are called *accessory dwelling units* in single-family zones. An accessory dwelling can be an apartment over a garage, a separate small structure on the same lot, or an apartment within the main house. They remain part of the original property, not subdivided from it. Some accessory dwellings can be legacies from the days of live-in servants, but they are becoming popular with local governments today as a way to open up single-family housing districts to some rental tenants who could not otherwise afford to live there.

Regulations for accessory dwellings limit their size, and often require that the landlord continue to live in the main house—a way of making sure that problem tenants will also be a problem for the property owner, not just the neighbors. While some owners may not want the headaches associated with being a landlord, the accessory dwelling unit can be a useful source of income, and sometimes a way of providing for family members. It can be easier to construct in neighborhoods with alleys or lanes, giving the second dwelling a separate means of access. However, the accessory unit can also be a wing added to the existing house, or a combined garage and apartment. Cities that permit these units have also created design standards for them, and each proposal is reviewed for compliance.[5]

Allowing a Mixture of Lot Sizes in Developing Areas

A residential zone in a typical zoning ordinance will permit, let us say, four houses to the acre. The way most ordinances accomplish this objective is to set a minimum lot size of ten thousand square feet, with four lots adding up to just short of the 43,560 square feet in an acre; the remaining space would probably be needed for a street. However, the objective of four units to the acre could also be accomplished without a minimum lot size, or a much smaller minimum lot size. If the minimum lot size were to be reduced to twenty-five hundred square feet, there could be four row houses on the acre, with the rest of the land left deeded as shared open space. Or there could be two larger lots of fifteen thousand square feet, and two smaller lots of five thousand square feet each. And so on, there are many permutations. These calculations become much more meaningful if they are applied to a typical development tract of fifty or one hundred acres. What is called *planned unit development* (PUD) permits such a relaxation of the minimum lot size, but only on a case-by-case basis after an official public process that takes as much time, and needs as many public hearings and approvals, as rezoning the property.

Simply getting rid of or reducing the minimum lot size, while keeping the overall density calculation, can eliminate the "cookie-cutter" subdivisions that characterize suburban development, where all the houses and lots in an entire development are the same size. Instead, there could be a mix of housing types, some more affordable, and the design of the development could be made both more walkable and more sustainable because a mix of different lot sizes allows more flexible designs for streets, which can then be designed to adapt to the natural topography. The changed regulations could also sometimes leave parts of the tract in a natural state, instead of making it necessary to develop the entire property in order to obtain the number of lots permitted by zoning.[6] There should be design review of such proposals by the local government, but the process could be "by right," not the complex rezoning procedure needed for a PUD exception.

Up-zoning commercial corridors for multifamily and row house development; assembling substantial tracts of now-vacant land in older cities and marketing them for development; permitting carefully selected and reviewed urban-infill sites at higher densities in established residential neighborhoods; permitting accessory dwelling units in existing neighborhoods; and allowing a range of lot sizes in new residential zones could—collectively—make megaregions far more equitable places, and reduce the need to urbanize more and more land. These are all measures that are feasible in today's real estate markets and do not require government subsidies. What is needed is to implement these changes throughout a megaregion, not just in a few special locations.

CHAPTER 9:

Adapting Governmental Structures to Manage Megaregions

Fragmentation of authority among counties, cities, towns, school districts, sewer districts, and other separate jurisdictions is typical of the emerging megaregions; they each include many of these overlapping clusters of governments. So how can governmental decisions be made for megaregions in order to protect the natural environment, adapt to climate change, reduce social inequities, and balance transportation?

The powers of all local governments and special districts derive from the states, so states will have to be primary actors in managing the emerging megaregions. When a megaregion is entirely within a single state, as in California, Florida, and Texas, the state's potential role is clear. Where megaregions cross state lines, an interstate compact may prove to be appropriate. The National Center for Interstate Compacts, part of the Council of State Governments, assists states in managing more than two hundred of these compacts created for many different purposes.

Managing Environmental Issues

Many governmental organizations could help make development more compatible with the natural environment if enabled by the states.

Multistate Compacts to Manage Watersheds: Watersheds have natural environmental boundaries, and the way they divide the landscape is rather like Russian nesting dolls. The Mississippi River watershed includes tributaries such as the Ohio River. The Ohio is formed at the confluence of the Monongahela and Allegheny River watersheds. These watersheds, in turn, have their own tributary rivers with their smaller watersheds, all the way down to ephemeral brooks and streams that flow only after exceptionally heavy rains. The great naturalist John Wesley Powell, in his analysis of lands in the American West, proposed in 1878 that state boundaries, or at the very least county boundaries, conform to watersheds. Much of the western land being divided into states had serious water shortages even then.[1] Powell reasoned that competition for water resources would be more manageable if the flow of water corresponded to governmental boundaries. Good advice: obviously not followed. But watersheds remain a major physical influence, and over the years, governments have found ways to relate development to them.

Under the US Constitution, states may form compacts with other states only with the consent of Congress.[2] Multistate compacts to manage watersheds have a long history, which provides examples of how environmental issues in megaregions can be managed. Multistate watershed management has been needed to ensure supplies of drinkable water and to minimize damage from flooding. In the dryer western states, allocation of water resources for all uses has been the dominant issue.

The Colorado River Compact is an early example. It was approved by the Congress in 1921 and signed in 1922 by Colorado, New Mexico, Utah, and Wyoming—where the upper division of the watershed is located—and Arizona, California, and Nevada, where the lower division is located.[3] The compact allocates water resources among the states. There is also a treaty allocating some of the Colorado River flow to Mexico. It has not solved the region's water-allocation problems, which have been a continual source of conflict and litigation, partly because the original estimates of available water resources turn out to be too high.

Other multistate water-management organizations that have been approved by Congress include the Interstate Environmental Commission (parts of New York, New Jersey, and Connecticut around New York City) in 1936; the Interstate Commission on the Potomac River Basin in 1940; the New England Interstate Water Pollution Control Commission in 1947; the Ohio River Valley Water Sanitation Commission in 1948; the Great Lakes Commission in 1955, the Delaware River Basin Commission in 1961; the Susquehanna River Basin Commission in 1970; the Upper Mississippi River Basin Association in 1981; the Columbia River Gorge Commission in 1987, and the Great Lakes–Saint Lawrence River Basin Water Resources Compact in 2005, which includes parts of Canada.

These organizations vary in their purposes and administrative structures, but they all were created because their watersheds extend across regular governmental boundaries; and drinking water supplies, flood control, and water pollution control cannot be managed without these agreements.

Coastal Zone Management: Coastal zone management is another environmental area where states operate a regional authority, in this case with coordination from the federal government. The US Congress passed the Coastal Zone Management Act in 1972. It covers all the coastal areas in the United States, including those along the Great Lakes. Although coastal zones are not watersheds, they include the river mouths and estuaries of watersheds; and coastal zones, like watersheds, extend across state boundaries and include many different jurisdictions.

Thirty-five states have coastlines that make them eligible to be included. Participation by the states is voluntary, and Alaska withdrew in 2011, the only eligible state that is not participating.[4] Within the provisions of the act, each state has the freedom to write its own regulations and procedures. While states generally delegate land-use decisions to local governments, the coastal zone management commissions derive their regulatory power from the state and can set parameters for local decision-making or even overrule a local government. The management role is changing from preserving environmentally sensitive coastal areas to evaluating development proposals as to whether coastal lands will be endangered by rising seas. In the future, coastal zone management commissions are likely to find themselves advising states that some coastal areas are no longer appropriate for habitation.

Statewide Watershed Management: Individual states have also created water-management districts based on natural boundaries. Florida, for example, has divided the state into five water-management districts, based primarily on watersheds, to administer the water supply, water quality, floodplain management and protection, as well as the preservation of natural systems.

Local Watershed Management Districts: Tulsa, Oklahoma, suffered a series of devastating floods from the Arkansas River. In 1985, Tulsa created a Department of Stormwater Management, and the next year enacted a citywide stormwater utility fee that all property owners must pay. These funds pay for stormwater- and flood-control projects and landscape preservation programs. Tulsa has revised its regulations so that a watershed development permit must be obtained before construction, landfill, or excavation in the floodplain; and new buildings must be elevated at least one foot above the floodplain as defined in the regulations. Any construction outside the floodplain but close to a natural or constructed watercourse also requires a permit. If there is a demonstrable need, these kinds of taxes, regulations, and permits are within the powers of all local governments.

Water and Sewer Districts: Water and sewer districts are usually watershed-based, for the simple reason that water flows downhill and has to be pumped over ridgelines. Currently the engineers working for these districts tend to see their role as figuring out how to implement decisions made by planning and zoning commissions, rather than telling the planning authorities what the best practices should be. Water supplies and sewage-treatment plants are a big part of the infrastructure of urban growth. Without these systems, new building must rely on private wells and septic tanks, which work only where development density is relatively low. Reliable water supplies and wastewater treatment should be designed to enable urban growth in the locations that are determined through regulations to be most suitable for development, rather than being the servant of economic trends initiated by real estate investors and passively accepted by cities and towns.

The Tennessee Valley Authority: The Tennessee Valley Authority (TVA) was created by the federal government in 1933. The authority controls land throughout the entire watershed of the Tennessee River, which includes the watersheds of tributary rivers that originate in Alabama, Georgia, Mississippi, North Carolina, and Virginia, as well as including the portion of Kentucky where the Tennessee River joins the Ohio River at Paducah.

Harnessing the whole watershed by building dams to generate electric power was a primary purpose of the authority. Hydroelectric power was intended to be an economic stimulus for a poverty-stricken area that had been even harder hit by the Great Depression. The reengineering of the rivers was also intended to improve flood control and navigation. Extending the power grid to rural areas that had never had electricity before was reinforced by programs advising farmers how to make their land more productive.

Making such extensive changes to a river system would be controversial today, now that ecological consequences of such interventions are better understood, but at the time, dam-building was widely accepted as good use of the opportunities nature provides. During World War II, many defense industries located in the Tennessee Valley to take advantage of cheap and abundant electricity, and the regional economy has been successful ever since.

Today the TVA has essentially become a very big public utility, operating coal-fired and nuclear-powered plants as well as providing hydroelectricity. However, the agency owns and manages 293,000 acres, and is also a steward of the natural environment: managing the water supply and keeping water quality high are important authority policies. These objectives mean regulating land use on authority lands and also using the authority's influence when local governments make land-use decisions.

It is unlikely that creating another TVA will be politically possible, but it remains a precedent for using watershed or other boundaries in designing a multistate region to manage both economic development and the environment.

Transportation Planning Is Already Regional

Each state has a department of transportation, and as mentioned earlier, the Federal Highway Act of 1962 has mandated metropolitan planning organizations (MPOs) for every metropolitan area in the country. Federal funds for highways and transit are meant to be used in accordance with plans drawn up by each state and the MPO for each metropolitan region.

These organizations are councils of governments, sometimes called COGs, where each local government is represented on the council, and there is a staff with an executive director. Resource-allocation decisions by MPOs about highway or transit funds are binding, although the state department of transportation is likely to have a big influence. Most of the other decisions of an MPO are advisory, but the COGs have been the only agencies planning for a whole region.

The Association of Bay Area Governments, founded in 1961, was a prototype MPO, created a year before the 1962 Federal Highway Act was passed. It is a COG for the nine counties and 101 cities and towns of the San Francisco Bay region. It is the MPO and it also prepares regional plans, and provides research to its member governments about land use, environmental- and water-resource protection, disaster resilience, energy efficiency, and hazardous-waste mitigation.

There is a national Association of Metropolitan Planning Organizations, and there are also statewide associations of MPOs in Arizona, Florida, Georgia, Illinois, New York State, North Carolina, Texas, Oregon, and West Virginia. When megaregions are contained within a single state, as in Florida, Texas, and California, the MPOs are already positioned to work together managing transportation issues that extend throughout a megaregion.

Where the megaregion extends beyond state boundaries, there can be interstate compacts about rail, water, and highway transportation. The Port Authority of New York and New Jersey is a well-known example. As mentioned in chapter 6, there is a Midwest Interstate Passenger Rail Compact, which could be a prototype for other agreements about railroads.

Can Megaregions Have a Regional Government?

There are a few US examples of consolidated government at the scale of the metropolitan region. Beginning in 1967, the Minneapolis–Saint Paul region has had a regional government, the Metropolitan Council, whose members are appointed by the governor of Minnesota. The Metropolitan Council's jurisdiction is contained within the state of Minnesota, and the state has the power to make regional decisions, and override local governments. That power, given to the Metropolitan Council, allows it to manage regional services that local governments cannot deliver as well on their own, including the regional transit system, regional wastewater treatment, a regional park system, tax-base sharing, and a housing program for low-income people across the metropolitan area.

The Metropolitan Council also prepares regional policy plans, including planning for future transit, wastewater management, and drinking water supplies. The regional government includes seven counties, many smaller cities and townships, plus special-purpose districts, like school districts.

Today, however, the Minneapolis–Saint Paul region has outgrown the boundaries established for the Metropolitan Council. The Minneapolis–Saint Paul–Bloomington metropolitan statistical area includes nine counties in addition to the seven participating in the Metropolitan Council: two in Wisconsin and seven more in Minnesota. The Metropolitan Council is still an effective regional government, but it no longer includes the whole region.[5]

The Portland, Oregon, metropolitan region also has its Metro government, which is elected, unlike the Metropolitan Council for the Twin Cities, but, as mentioned in chapter 1, the area it covers has a conspicuous exception. Vancouver, Washington, is right across the Columbia River from Portland, and is definitely part of the metropolitan region, but as it is in a different state, it is not part of Portland Metro. Other metropolitan regions in the United States have not been able to overcome similar divisions of authority and create a regional government.

Counties, found in most states, generally govern an area that is bigger than the individual city, although many major cities are part of consolidated city-county governments, and New York City is composed of five counties. Miami-Dade County includes the cities of Miami and Miami Beach, as well as other communities. It covers about a third of the Greater Miami region and is an example of successful governance at a regional scale.

States have the power to create regional governments, but doing this is up to governors and legislators, who listen to mayors, town boards, and county commissions. Getting local governments to cede part of their powers to a regional authority bigger than a county in order to create new governments for megaregions, even if the new government were to control only a few sets of issues, will take a long time—especially if the megaregion spans state lines and requires a multistate organization similar to the Tennessee Valley Authority. Such efforts may never succeed at all. It will be more effective to leave a megaregional government to be a long-term possibility and, in the meantime, deal with urgent current issues using existing institutions.

Development Suitability Can Set the Boundaries for Megaregions

State governments all have planning agencies. Using information from proprietary geographic information systems (GIS), from coastal zone management commissions—if they cover parts of the megaregion—and data compiled by the Landscape Conservation Cooperatives described in chapter 3, states can compile maps of development suitability for the areas at the perimeters of existing development. Suitability includes the position of the land within a watershed, the sensitivity of soils and vegetation to destabilization by development, but also the likelihood of problems created by a changing climate, such as coastal flooding, seasonal flooding from rivers, flash floods from local downpours, and wildfire. These are objective bases for making location decisions for development and infrastructure.

The next step for the state planning agency is to prepare projections of development trends, as shown on maps like the one in chapter 3 (figure 3-2), which can be compared with maps of suitability for development, a relatively easy operation to perform, now that GIS maps are available. The planning agency, or individual MPOs, can then propose a growth boundary based on development suitability, but also on a budget of the land needed to accommodate projected development, as is done in administering growth boundaries in Oregon. Determining the size of the land budget will be one of the biggest political problems. Development suitability will require more irregular shapes than a conventional growth boundary, with some parts of the potential development zone extending farther from existing development than others.

The argument for this process is not just about preserving the natural environment from destabilization—it is also about saving public money. Not building more roads and utilities than will be needed is one category of savings; another comes from money not spent on disaster relief by keeping new development out of harm's way. These are arguments that will be important for state legislators when they are considering a growth boundary proposal.

Where the megaregion crosses state boundaries, states can coordinate their management of growth boundaries, can use an existing interstate compact, or can create an interstate compact that includes an entire megaregion. It can be similar to the interstate regional compacts that already exist to manage watersheds and follow a similar model of having a governing council representing all parts of the megaregion, and a staff that can make plans and coordinate actions.

A Balanced Transportation System Can Organize Development within the Megaregion Growth Boundary

The routes and stations for fast-enough trains and transit systems that have their own rights-of-way can facilitate growth in the parts of the megaregion that are most suitable for new development, and also channel growth to bypassed areas in older urban centers and along the commercial corridors where land uses are changing because of e-retail. Determining these routes is the province of state departments of transportation, but also of the MPOs established across every state. The state and the MPOs should take advantage of new GIS capabilities and use development-suitability maps in determining highway and transit routes, as access is such an important driver of future development.

Where a megaregion is entirely within one state, there can be an alliance of MPOs, such as the Florida Metropolitan Planning Organization Advisory Council, which covers almost the whole state. The MPOAC produces a Strategic Direction Plan and a Unified Planning Work Program. If there is not already an association of MPOs, one can be formed to coordinate transportation decisions across the megaregion. Again, an existing interstate compact can be adapted to coordinate transportation for the megaregion, or a new one can be created.

States Can Set Policies for Local Regulations

States delegated the power to make land-use decisions, within the context of property rights, to local governments because most of the information needed to make these decisions could be found only at the local level, if it existed at all. Today, GIS information gives the states the ability to set the framework for local decision-making about land suitability, and the states can also determine the basic configuration of growth boundaries.

States already determine transportation frameworks. States and regional compacts have both the power and the information to overrule local governments on such issues, should they find it necessary. However, most of the consequential decisions about development in megaregions will continue to be made by local governments, which will remain the most suitable place for implementation decisions to be made because so many of the often conflicting politics are local.

Changes can be made to local development regulations to make well-informed decisions that affect the environment, transportation, and equity and are in harmony with basic principles established by the states for the megaregions. For cities, suburbs, and towns to decide issues in ways that support the megaregion, changes to the way that local zoning and subdivision codes are written and administered will be required. This is the subject of the next chapter.

CHAPTER 10:

Rewriting Local Regulations to Promote Sustainability and Equity

Local regulations control the physical shape and structure of cities, suburbs, and towns by determining how, when, and where real estate development occurs, and defining the legal rights of property owners. These regulations also have a huge effect on the natural environment, on whether or not an area can have the densities needed to support transit, and in many places, development regulations have been a way to institutionalize discrimination. While states and multistate compacts now have the ability to set detailed policies for growth management, implementation of these policies will largely be through development regulations written and administered by local governments.

Zoning and subdivision, the principal components of local development regulations, originated in the United States in the 1920s. Most local governments amended their regulations in the 1960s in response to new concepts favored by influential law and planning schools. Rules were changed to control the size of buildings by a ratio of permitted space to the size of the lot, in addition to the height limits and setbacks from the edge of the property that had been the basic controls before. Zoning maps were amended to make more distinctions among different types of real estate development; and subdivision standards—which regulate street designs and lot sizes in new developments—became much more detailed and precise. At the same time that the rules became stricter and more complicated, a procedure called planned unit development (PUD) was added that permitted local authorities to make exceptions to some of the rules for larger properties on the basis of an actual development plan.

Two generations later, almost all zoning and subdivision regulations are now out of date. They do not relate well to the current real estate market, to the development needs created by population growth in the megaregions around the country, to an economy changing rapidly in response to advances in telecommunication and transportation networks, and to changes in climate that, over time, will alter the natural environment in which development takes place.[1]

Many people have concluded that managing development at the scale of the megaregions is impossible, particularly because zoning and subdivision regulations are adopted and administered by cities and towns, and sometimes counties, and there are hundreds of these local governments in every megaregion—each with its own political and economic concerns. But as we have seen, states have the power to set the framework for development regulations, and they now have the information to enable them to do this.

Development regulations have the potential to help solve the megaregions' pressing growth-management and environmental problems. While every local set of regulations is different, they contain many similarities because they are based on widely shared templates. Revising only a few critical aspects of zoning and subdivision will go a long way toward addressing the biggest impediments to designing the megaregion, without disturbing the way other parts of the regulatory system affect most of the land area of cities, towns, and suburbs. The changes are relatively simple to enact. Most jurisdictions could make the necessary changes on their own, and the changes could also be mandated by state governments through their enabling legislation.

Relating Development to the Natural Environment

The natural environment is a blind spot in most development regulations, which are written as if land were a flat tabletop. At the time these regulations were first enacted, accurate mapping of environmental features was not available at the scale of a whole community, and nature was seen as a set of conditions that could be subdued and adapted by engineering.

Adding Environmental Information to Zoning Maps: The typical zoning map in use today is not very different from the first zoning maps used in the 1920s, even if it appears on a computer screen and not just on paper. It is a street map with an overlay showing the boundaries of the various zones. It may also show property lines. Almost all local governments now have geographic information systems (GIS) capable of producing a much more informative map. The states can also convey environmental information and studies of potential future development to local governments, which can also obtain detailed information from many other sources.

The layers of a GIS-based zoning map could include an aerial photograph, building shapes, tree cover, land contours, the locations of ponds and streams, the official hundred-year and five-hundred-year floodplains, and soil types—all information that was not readily available when the format for zoning maps was first established. On a computer, selected layers of GIS information can be read together or separately. Local governments reviewing a zoning application can, and do, ask for a survey from the developer. But that survey covers only one property, and the zoning process has been blind to the off-site consequences of the decisions being made.

As discussed in chapter 3, the quality of GIS-based environmental information is now good enough that local governments can rely on it for decision-making. Authorities can make an administrative decision to add to their zoning maps relevant environmental information from their GIS system, and from growth management boundaries generated by the state, by regional agencies, or MPOs. Planning departments can also use this information to prepare environmental conservation plans for their whole community, and these plans can be the basis for adding environmental overlay zones to the regulations.

A priority environmental overlay would be flood-zone maps combining the hundred-year and five-hundred-year floodplains together with the streams in local watershed systems. The downstream consequences for other property owners can then be estimated when considering zoning and subdivision approvals. The ability of local governments to enact official environmental zones may depend on their state enabling legislation. Where they don't have this authority, the state laws can be amended.

Preventing development from damaging the interests of other property owners is a central reason why development regulations were adopted, which is a strong argument for adding environmental protections to the regulations. Environmental zones can be enacted and mapped that restrict the kind and amount of development that can take place where the natural environment is especially sensitive to disruption. These zones need to be based on objective considerations and implement a comprehensive environmental protection plan.

Removing Incentives for Environmental Damage from Residential Subdivision: Dividing a property into residential lots is regulated by the subdivision ordinance. When a developer cuts down all the trees and then flattens the land with a bulldozer, it is easy to blame the developer for the inevitable erosion and flooding that follow such a disturbance to the natural equilibrium. But the developer may well be responding to legal requirements. The subdivision regulations set maximum grades for streets; one standard is meant to fit all properties. The zoning code sets minimum sizes for lots. To develop the land to its legal maximum and get access to all the potential lots, the easiest course is to simply reengineer the land until it meets the requirements. The PUD exception offers the developer the chance to propose alternatives more suitable to the local topography, but applying is complicated, may arouse community opposition, and will take time. A developer may just not bother with it.

Some of the exceptions possible with PUD can and should be made available by right. The zone in which the property is located sets the number of house lots per acre. That is usually enforced by setting a minimum lot size. If the code says four houses per acre will be permitted, the minimum lot size will be a quarter of an acre. But the four-houses-per-acre requirement can remain, and, as discussed in chapter 8, the minimum lot size can be reduced to, let us say, the size of a town house lot, about one-sixteenth of an acre—or any size in between. But still only four houses to the acre, which could occupy a smaller portion of the land. The developer then has much more flexibility in laying out the streets. There can also be provisions that permit steeper streets, as long as the configuration of intersections continues to meet the requirements.

Subdivision plans require review and approval, so the local government retains control of the process. Reducing the minimum lot size while keeping the density requirement can also be a way of permitting more affordable housing. We will come back to this possibility later in this chapter.

Green Parking Lots: A big cause of flash flooding is rapid runoff of rain from large parking lots, because the paving does not absorb water. Reflected heat from parking lots is also a cause of "islands" of more intense heat during the summer. Regulations for keeping the slope of the parking lot within predetermined percentages can also result in bull-dozing of large areas.

Large parking lots on sloping sites can be divided in a series of ter-races that each meet the grading requirements and are connected by short ramps. This should be a relatively simple regulatory change, as it is an alternative way of meeting the existing requirements and not dif-ficult to implement. Heat islands can be mitigated by requiring shade trees of a specified minimum size planted as a ratio to the number of cars, either at the ends of rows of parked cars, between the rows of cars, or at the periphery of a smaller lot. The car spaces themselves can be required to be paved in one of the new products that have a con-tinuous, seamless surface but permit rainwater to flow through to the underlying soil.

Again, adding landscaping requirements for parking lots is not a major change in existing practice. These revised regulations should apply to all new parking lots, but also to any parking lot where there is a significant change in the associated building. Over time, green parking lots can have a strong favorable influence on local microclimates.

Adapting to Climate Change Locally

Regardless of the future success of controlling greenhouse gases in the atmosphere, warming trends will continue to change the climate for decades. Understanding how to adapt to these new conditions is a criti-cal component in managing the growth of megaregions.

Wildfire: As mentioned in chapter 2, one-third of all residences in the United States are within the wildland–urban interface; that is, they are in danger of burning if the nearby forest catches fire. Right now most of the problems with wildfire are in the far West, but figure 2-4 on page 23 shows that the majority of places that could be at risk in the future are east of the Mississippi River. This part of the country receives much more rainfall than the West, but warmer temperatures and lon-ger hot seasons, which are making existing forests less adapted to their location, are beginning to cause trees to start dying in the East. Over time, forests will adapt to new conditions, but during the transition, they will be susceptible to burning. Much of the East was built on land cleared of forests, and the forests have come back and are interwoven with the developed areas.

Local communities need to map their wildland–urban interface, as defined in the US Healthy Forest Restoration Act of 2003, and communities should also prepare a wildfire-protection plan, working with the US Forest Service and Bureau of Land Management when the forests are federally owned. While the US law calls only for voluntary compliance with the protection plan, the states can make compliance mandatory, and local governments can incorporate such plans into development regulations. They can use the zoning code to map fire-risk zones, and the building code to require fire-resistant construction and an area clear of flammable plantings around buildings located in these zones. There is also the much more difficult question of whether some fire-risk zones should not permit residences or buildings occupied by many people, like hospitals, schools, and office buildings.[2]

Storm Surges and River Floods: Recent river floods have been demonstrating that existing dikes and flood walls may not be able to withstand the higher floodwaters from the increased rainfall that accompanies a warmer climate. More frequent and more intense hurricanes are also a likely part of climate change. Hurricane Katrina in 2005 showed what storm surges could do to New Orleans and the Gulf Coast, and storm surges from not-quite-a-hurricane Sandy caused devastation in New York City, Long Island, and along the New Jersey and Connecticut coasts in 2012.

Relying on insurance becomes less effective as flood events become more frequent. At some point, insurance can become either impossibly expensive or completely unavailable. Beyond insurance, the first line of defense against river floods and storm surges ought to be collective protection using constructed or natural barriers along with pump systems, and paid for by government, not individual property owners.

The local government can also map flood-protection zones to make sure that individual buildings are as flood-resistant as possible. The building code can require that, for buildings in flood zones, mechanical systems be located on rooftops, not in basements, and that structures can withstand a storm.

The Federal Emergency Management Agency (FEMA) maps should be incorporated in zoning, as FEMA requires minimum heights above ground level for inhabited floors (which can require that whole houses or other buildings be raised) and also regulates how much a building can obstruct a flood surge in velocity zones.[3]

Over time, some local governments will have to confront the question of whether there are parts of the city that should not be zoned for inhabited buildings. Norfolk, Virginia, is beginning to deal with this issue, as discussed on page 17 in chapter 2. Where state plans have shown areas to be at risk from floods or wildfire, local governments should be prevented by the states from approving development in such at-risk areas.

Supporting Both Equity and Transportation by Mixing Land Uses and Housing Types

Remapping commercial corridors to a zone that also permits multifamily housing and row houses is a concept introduced in chapter 8. The rezoning provides a way to reuse retail properties that are becoming obsolete because of e-commerce.

Rezoning commercial corridors can open up neighborhoods and suburbs that are primarily single-family houses to more affordable town houses and apartments. This housing can benefit people already living in the area who wish to downsize or find a home for family members, or who work in the community but can't afford to live there. A percentage of this housing can be subsidized, which can create choices for people who want to move out from the inner city but can't afford a single-family house, or even a suburban apartment. Raising the density in these corridors to something like ten families to the acre can create a viable market for a transit line, probably bus rapid transit, which does not require the level of capital investment that would be needed for rail transit but can provide a comparable service.

Given the revolution currently going on in retail, it makes sense for communities to permit apartments and row houses in other commercial zones. Adding apartments to business centers can help create walkable mixed-use districts, which can be preferred places to live, as well as reinforcing office uses and providing more customers for shops and restaurants.

Row houses and apartments are currently being built out at the urban fringe, because it has been difficult to find suitable sites in established suburban communities. Opening more opportunities to build closer to traditional suburban and urban centers can take some of the development pressure off the edges of suburbia—making it easier to preserve the landscape and saving some of the cost of infrastructure and services that would otherwise be needed.

Metropolitan planning organizations would be a good forum for coordinating the rezoning of commercial corridors that run through multiple communities, and funding the transit necessary to serve them.

Inclusionary Zoning: Zoning regulations have helped institutionalize segregated neighborhoods by using minimum lot sizes to differentiate residential zones. States and cities are beginning to address these housing inequalities.

What the press has called "eliminating single-family zoning" has recently become policy in Minneapolis and is the basis for a new law in Oregon; other states and cities are looking at similar measures.

Eliminating needs to be put in quotes, as single-family houses continue to be legal, and new ones can still be built. In Oregon the change is to permit duplex housing units on what had been single-family lots in cities above ten thousand people, and up to four units will be permitted on some single-family lots in cities of more than twenty-five thousand people and in the Portland Metro area. In Minneapolis the adopted policy is to permit three housing units to be built on formerly single-family lots. These initiatives are intended to increase the supply of affordable housing and remove barriers that have kept lower-income people from living in large parts of cities and suburbs.

The big effect of allowing four units on a single-family lot is not going to be felt in neighborhoods of million-dollar homes. If it costs $1 million to acquire a property, and the developer intends to rebuild four houses or apartments, each will have to sell for $1 million to meet the typical real estate practice that the cost of land acquisition should not be more than a quarter of the purchase price. If fewer new units are permitted, the purchase price of new development will need to be even higher. However, if the acquisition cost of a house and lot is $200,000, four new units would need to be priced at only $200,000. These numbers tell us that the impact of permitting more units in single-family zones will occur mostly in modest areas where people might rent or own an older, small house on a lot that is big enough for redevelopment.

How the new development is managed will make a big difference for the future of these neighborhoods. A hands-off policy for denser development in established neighborhoods will be destructive as well as unpopular. The Toronto regulations mentioned on page 115 are a good example of a way to increase residential density in an established neighborhood by setting standards and reviewing proposals.

The option for an another, smaller dwelling unit on a single-family lot, either as part of the main house or a variation on what used to be called a garage apartment, is being added to the regulations in many cities. Again, standards and a review process can help maintain and enhance the good aspects of the existing neighborhood.

Mixing lot sizes within a zone, as mentioned earlier, makes it easier to lay out a subdivision without destructive stripping of vegetation and regrading taking place over an entire property. It also makes it possible to integrate more affordable housing within development as it takes place. The overall density requirement in residential units per acre remains the same and is enforceable when plans are reviewed for subdivision approval and continues to be enforceable when building permits are applied for. What changes is the minimum lot size, which could be reduced, for example, to one-sixteenth of an acre, the size of a typical row house lot. It would be much easier to preserve parts of the land that should not be built on, and the developer could easily end up spending less money on streets and other infrastructure. It would also be easier to design a walkable community, as some of the dwellings would be closer together, and it would also be easier to set aside a percentage of the units as subsidized housing. The normal approval process for a subdivision includes extensive review by the planning authorities. That review process should remain in place, and there ought to be standards for walkable mixed-lot-size communities to guide the review process.

Changes like those outlined in this chapter ought to be within the existing powers of most local governments. They are central to implementing an improved design for megaregions.

A Design Agenda
for Megaregions

As megaregions grow to the population and economic importance predicted for them by 2050, we have seen that three new initiatives can reshape current trends into a regional design. Work can begin right now, using government institutions that already exist and development concepts that make sense in today's real estate market. Implementing this design agenda can begin in parts of a megaregion, and successes in one place can help start the process elsewhere.

Detailed information about the natural environment needs to be available in geographic information systems (GIS) at every level of government. Decision-makers can then use this information to be certain that the evolving megaregions will fit safely into their environmental setting and avoid locations that are becoming hazardous because of a warming climate.

Passenger rail service running through each of the developing megaregions can be upgraded to the level of the Acela service in the Northeast. While intercity trains are only one component of a balanced transportation system, and walking, cycling, driving, transit, and airplane travel will continue to be important—and will also need improvements—the lesson from Amtrak's Northeast Corridor is that fast-enough train service can reduce both congestion within the air-travel system and gridlock on the highways.

Local development regulations should be changed to counteract past government policies that have made megaregions very unequal places. The two most important changes will be opening suburban commercial corridors to multifamily housing and changing some of the ways individual houses are controlled by zoning.

If you are convinced that implementing these changes is important, a good place to start is your local zoning board or planning commission. They have the power to adopt zoning maps that include GIS information, to rezone commercial corridors, and to amend their development regulations to reduce minimum lot sizes and permit accessory dwelling units. If you want legal and technical backup for advocating these amendments to zoning and subdivision regulations, you can consult Brian Blaesser's and my *Reinventing Development Regulations*, published by the Lincoln Institute of Land Policy. This book can be downloaded from Lincoln's website free as a PDF or EPUB book.

If you belong to a civic organization, an advocacy group like the Sierra Club or the Congress for the New Urbanism, or a professional organization such as the US Green Building Council, the American Planning Association, the American Society of Landscape Architects, the American Institute of Architects, or the Urban Land Institute, you can work to reinforce policies they may already have toward implementing the agenda for megaregions, including balancing transportation.

And of course, if you are part of the professional staff or a board member of the many governmental agencies that share the power to implement this agenda, you can work to make it happen.

Here is a summary of actions needed to make the changes described in this book:

Use GIS to Inform Policy Decisions with Environmental Implications

States, their coastal zone management agencies, and the multistate compacts that manage watersheds have powers that would allow them to reshape development within critical ecoregions. They have not done nearly so much as is needed, because they lacked the necessary detailed environmental information, which has been available only to local governments, and then almost always only for individual properties where development was being proposed. Local governments have not been able to base their regulatory policies on environmental considerations, because they, too, lacked the necessary information. Environmental impact studies, where required, have been focused on individual proposals.

Geographic information systems provide the ability to incorporate an understanding of soils, land contours, vegetation, water flows, floodplains, and other natural features at the scale of regional watersheds and coastlines. Because the technology is new, its usefulness in making important policy decisions is only now being understood.

The twenty-two Landscape Conservation Cooperatives established in 2010 across the United States, funded and coordinated by the Fish and Wildlife Service of the US Department of the Interior, are becoming an important source of conservation designs that include environmental information in GIS. Environmental information is also readily available from proprietary sources.

The new technology makes it possible to map predicted development trends in GIS and compare them with the environmental maps. Future floodplains, wildland–urban interfaces, areas of potential heat concentration, and similar considerations can also be mapped and compared with predicted development trends as shown in chapter 3. Places that are inappropriate for development can be mapped, and regulations used to guide development to other areas.

In addition to local planning and zoning boards and commissions, Metropolitan Planning Organizations, state planning agencies, and the interstate compacts that administer watersheds are among the governmental entities that should map environmental resources, project future development trends, and then guide the growth of megaregions to locations that will not destabilize the natural environment, and away from places that are becoming unsafe because of a changing climate. This process will need to be repeated at intervals, as the regulations will change the development trends. Because government has gained this ability to safeguard the public interest in development, it now also has the responsibility to use it.

Build Fast-Enough Trains

The United States ought to give priority to building a high-speed rail network comparable to those within Europe and China. There is no current political prospect for doing this. However, existing passenger rail lines connect the major cities within all the emerging megaregions.

Upgrading passenger trains to the level provided by Amtrak's Acela service is technically feasible and—compared to building Chinese- or European-style high-speed rail—inexpensive. The money spent will continue to be a good investment for shorter trips even if higher-speed trains are eventually put into service. Tracks need to be improved to support faster speeds, grade crossings gated or eliminated, and the lines electrified.

Private investors have recently shown an interest in providing improved passenger train service, notably the Virgin Trains USA service operating in Florida and projected for other areas. Amtrak by statute has priority over freight trains along rail corridors shared with freight operators, a condition of Amtrak's taking over passenger service from the other rail lines. Amtrak is thus likely to be an indispensable partner for private investors in upgrading passenger rail service. It is also important that private investors work with Amtrak and state governments and not monopolize the parts of the megaregion where train service is likely to be most profitable, such as the segment from Atlanta to Charlotte within the corridor from Birmingham to Raleigh.

States have the power to negotiate with Amtrak and private investors to implement better regional passenger service. A model for how states can fund the necessary improvements to permit fast-enough trains is the interstate compact among states creating improved rail service between Chicago and Detroit and the State of Michigan's actions to support this plan, as described in chapter 6. To be fully effective in reshaping regional development, fast-enough trains need to connect to major airports and to local rapid transit systems.

Address Inequality in Local Zoning

States and cities are beginning to address the housing inequalities that can be produced by local regulations. In Oregon a new law requires duplex housing units to be permitted on what had been single-family lots in cities above ten thousand people, and up to four units on some single-family lots in cities of more than twenty-five thousand people and in the Portland Metro area. In Minneapolis the adopted policy is to permit three housing units to be built on formerly single-family lots. These initiatives are intended to increase the supply of affordable housing and remove barriers that have kept lower-income people from living in large parts of cities and suburbs.

Oregon has left the details of implementing the new law to the individual cities. Portland has been studying how to manage such a change for some time. Critical variables include the size of the lot, parking requirements, and the way infill is designed. Toronto's guidelines for infill housing, as described in chapter 8, are useful in showing several different ways to manage increased housing density in established neighborhoods.

The big effect of allowing four units on a single-family lot is not going to be felt in neighborhoods of million-dollar homes, but in relatively modest areas where people might rent or own an older, small house on a lot that is big enough for redevelopment.

While Minnesota and Oregon have intervened to make comprehensive changes in local zoning regulations, local governments have several less sweeping options available to open up residential areas to more diverse kinds of houses and apartments. Many cities and towns now permit what is called an accessory dwelling unit on a single-family lot; and all local governments within the evolving megaregions should consider doing this as a simple way to help more people live in single-family neighborhoods. The size of the accessory apartment is generally limited, and it continues to belong to the primary owner, unlike a duplex, where the lot is subdivided. Adding smaller, and consequently more affordable, rental apartments to single-family houses has proved to be politically acceptable, because the profits belong to the local owners.

While single-family zoning has often been used as a means of exclusion, limiting density through zoning continues to be needed to keep new development synchronized with available utilities and government services. Keeping the zoned density, but reducing the minimum lot size, would make it possible to create neighborhoods of diverse housing types in developing areas, as explained in chapter 8.

Changing retail patterns are emptying out the commercial corridors that run like veins throughout megaregions. This land can, and should, be rezoned for attached houses and apartments, making development more diverse and taking some growth pressures off rural areas. Local governments can make affordable units part of the requirements for these new multifamily housing zones, following the model used successfully for many years by Montgomery County, Maryland. With more people living in these corridors, they can support bus rapid transit, creating opportunities to take some of the traffic off roads and highways.

While such land-use decisions will continue to be primarily the responsibility of local governments, actions to manage the development of the megaregions can be coordinated by the states, which are the source of all the regulatory powers administered by cities and towns. Where the megaregions are within a single state, as in Florida, Texas, or California, the coordination mechanism could be the state planning agency, or a council of metropolitan planning organizations, such as already exists in Florida. Where the megaregion extends across state lines, the mechanism could be an interstate compact, for which there are many possible models.

Individual citizens, civic organizations, advocacy groups, and professional organizations can influence government agencies to implement the megaregion design agenda, as can the staff and leadership of the agencies themselves. These improvements to the way decisions are made about megaregions will still leave many difficult choices to be made within the new framework. However, compared to current trends, adopting these practical and relatively simple changes will lead to a much more desirable future.

Illustration Credits

Figure 1-1: *America in 2050* project of the Regional Plan Association

Figure 1-2: Garrett Dash Nelson and Alisdair Rae, "An Economic Geography of the United States: From Commutes to Megaregions," *PLOS ONE* 11, no. 11 (2016): e0166083, https://doi.org/10.1371/journal.pone.0166083; used in accordance with Creative Commons License 4.0

Figure 2-1: Level III and IV Ecoregions in Washington, US Environmental Protection Agency

Figure 2-2: Photo by formulanone, used under Creative Commons License 2.0

Figure 2-3: Map from US Environmental Protection Agency data as compiled by James G. Titus and Charlie Richman

Figure 2-4: Wildland Urban Interface 2010; SILVIS Lab, University of Wisconsin–Madison

Figure 3-1: Southeast Blueprint v3.0, Southeast Conservation Adaptation Study, Southeast Conservation Adaptation Strategy, Matt Snider, February 2, 2019; Service Layer Credits: Copyright © 2013 by National Geographic Society, i-cubed

Figure 3-2: These data represent the extent of urbanization predicted by the model SLEUTH, developed by Dr. Keith C. Clarke at the University of California, Santa Barbara, Department of Geography and modified by David I. Doato of the United States Geological Survey Eastern Geographic Science Center; further model modification and implementation were performed at the Biodiversity and Spatial Information Center at North Carolina State University; Service Layer Credits: Copyright © 2013 by National Geographic Society, i-cubed

Figure 4-1: US Department of Transportation, Federal Highway Administration

Figure 4-2: Courtesy Skidmore, Owings & Merrill

Figure 5-1: US Federal Railroad Administration

Figure 5-2: California High-Speed Rail Authority

Figure 5-3: Map by Los Angeles Metrolink

Figure 5-4: Amtrak

Figure 6-1: Port Authority of New York and New Jersey

Figure 6-2: Photo by Mariordo, used under Creative Commons License 3.0

Figure 6-3: Photo by jim.henderson, used under Creative Commons License 1.0, public domain

Figure 7-1: Satellite view of Bridgeport, Connecticut; imagery Copyright © 2019 by Google; map data Copyright © 2019 by Google

Figure 7-2: NASA photo

Figure 7-3: NASA photo

Figure 8-1: Satellite view of Ellisville, Missouri; imagery Copyright © 2019 by Google; map data Copyright © 2019 by Google

Figure 8-2: Illustration by Friedman, Tung + Sasaki Urban Design, used by permission

Figure 8-3: City of Toronto

Notes

Chapter 1: A New Scale for Urban Challenges

1. According to figures from the 2010 census, 62.7 percent of the US population lives in incorporated areas. The census also counts another category of people living in small places that have a population density the Census Bureau considers urban but are within otherwise rural areas. Including these places brings the percentage of people living in urban areas to 80.7. These percentages are likely to go up when the 2020 census figures are analyzed.

2. Jean Gottmann, *Megalopolis: The Urbanized Northeastern Seaboard of the United States* (Cambridge, MA: MIT Press, 1961).

3. See "Identifying Megaregions in the United States: Implications for Infrastructure Investment" by Catherine L. Ross and Myungje Woo and "Megapolitan America: Defining and Applying a New Geography" by Robert E. Lang and Arthur C. Nelson in *Megaregions: Planning for Global Competitiveness*, edited by Catherine L. Ross (Washington, DC: Island Press, 2009).

4. This map is from the America in 2050 project of the Regional Plan Association.

5. Arthur Nelson and Robert Lang, *Megapolitan America* (London and New York: Routledge, 2013).

6. Garrett Dash Nelson and Alisdair Rae, "An Economic Geography of the

United States: From Commutes to Megaregions," *PLOS ONE* 11, no. 11 (2016): e0166083, https://doi.org/10.1371/journal.pone.0166083. The map is based on data from the American Community Survey by the United States Census Bureau. It corresponds well to the more intuitive megaregion maps based on current and projected population concentrations.

7. The US Congress in 2017 capped the federal tax deduction for local taxes at $10,000 and also reduced the amount of mortgage interest that can be deducted.

Chapter 2: Recognizing Ecoregions as the Context for Development

1. According to the EPA's Ecoregions webpage, this definition is based on a publication by James M. Omernik, "Ecoregions of the Conterminous United States," *Annals of the Association of American Geographers* 77, no. 1 (March 1987): 118–125.

2. Greater Miami-Dade County is featured on the 100 Resilient Cities website: www.100resilientcities.org/cities/greater-miami-and-the-beaches/.

3. See Sarah Almukhtar et al., "The Great Flood of 2019: A Complete Picture of a Slow-Motion Disaster," *New York Times*, September 11, 2019.

4. Volker C. Radeloff et al., "Rapid Growth of the US Wildland-Urban Interface Raises Wildfire Risk," *Proceedings of the National Academy of Sciences* 115, no. 13 (March 27, 2018): 3314–19, https://doi.org/10.1073/pnas.1718850115. Molly Mowery et al., *Planning the Wildland-Urban Interface*, Planning Advisory Service Report 594 (Chicago and Washington, DC: American Planning Association, 2019).

5. Dashka Slater, "Can Phoenix Remain Habitable?" *Sierra*, January 2019.

Chapter 3: Relating Development to the Natural Environment

1. A news story in *The Guardian* by Mallory Pickett on April 8, 2019, reported that the Trump administration has stopped funding the cooperatives, although the US Congress has appropriated their budgets.

2. Ian L. McHarg, *Design with Nature* (Garden City, NY: Natural History Press, 1969; New York: John Wiley & Sons, 1995).

3. Barry Commoner, *The Closing Circle: Nature, Man, and Technology* (New York: Knopf, 1971), 33–46.

4. Kendig described his proposal as "Performance Zoning," which is

confusing because his percentages are explicit requirements, and not defined by performance at all. Lane Kendig with Susan Connor, Cranston Byrd, and Judy Heyman, *Performance Zoning* (Chicago and Washington, DC: Planners Press, 1980).

5. For a discussion of how local governments can incorporate GIS information into zoning regulation, see *Reinventing Development Regulations* by the author and Brian W. Blaesser (Cambridge, MA: Lincoln Institute of Land Policy, 2017), particularly pages 17–21.

6. Ebenezer Howard, *To-morrow: A Peaceful Path to Real Reform* (London, Swan Sonnenschein & Co., Ltd., 1898). The 1902 and 1922 editions were titled *Garden Cities of To-morrow.*

7. See, for example, the account of Howard's influence in *City Design: Modernist, Traditional, Green and Systems Perspectives* by the author (London and New York: Routledge, 2016), second edition, pages 138–166.

8. A frank discussion of builder's costs can be found in magazines written for the housing industry. (See, for example, "Don't Pay Too Much for Land" by Chuck Shinn, in the June 2004 issue of *Professional Builder.*)

9. As tabulated on the *Kiplinger* website, updated January 2019: "Home Prices in the 100 Largest Metro Areas," https://www.kiplinger.com/tool /real-estate/T010-S003-home-prices-in-100-top-u-s-metro-areas/index .php.

Chapter 4: The Northeast Megaregion: Prototype for Balanced Transportation

1. Prediction from *Beyond Traffic 2045*, US Department of Transportation, draft, 2015.

2. Bruce Schaller, "In a Reversal, 'Car-Rich' Households Are Growing," *CityLab*, January 7, 2019.

3. Bruce Schaller, *Unsustainable? The Growth of App-Based Ride Services and Traffic, Travel and the Future of New York City*, Schaller Consulting, February 27, 2017, http://www.schallerconsult.com/rideservices/unsus tainable.pdf.

4. Gregory D. Erhardt et al., "Do Transportation Network Companies Decrease or Increase Congestion?," *Science Advances* 5, no. 5 (May 8, 2019).

5. "Amtrak's Next-Generation of High-Speed Trains," Amtrak, August 2016,

http://blog.amtrak.com/2016/08/amtraks-next-generation-high-speed
-trains/.

6. *Host Railroad Report Card & FAQ*, Amtrak, March 2018, http://media
.amtrak.com/wp-content/uploads/2018/03/CY2017-Report-Card-%E2
%80%93-FAQ-%E2%80%93-Route-Details.pdf.

Chapter 5: Progress Toward Fast-Enough Trains in Megaregions

1. From Article X, Section 19, of the Florida Constitution, enacted in 2000,
repealed in 2004.

2. Form S-1 Registration Statement under the Securities Act of 1933, Virgin
Trains USA LLC, November 16, 2018.

3. *2018 Business Plan*, California High-Speed Rail Authority, 38.

Chapter 6: Achieving Balanced Transportation in Megaregions

1. Some information about train speeds in this paragraph is drawn from a
High-Speed Rail Feasibility Study for the Rocky Mountain Rail Authority
by Quandel Consultants LLC, March 2010.

2. Bonnie Au, "China Unveils Ground-Breaking High-Speed Maglev Train
Prototype," *South China Morning Post*, May 16, 2019.

3. As of June 2019, Indiana decided not to fund the Hoosier State train service to and from Chicago.

4. "Amtrak and State Partners Reach Agreement to Preserve All Corridor
Routes," Amtrak, October 15, 2013.

5. *FAA Aerospace Forecasts: Fiscal Years 2018–2038*, Federal Aviation Administration, https://www.faa.gov/data_research/aviation/aerospace_forecasts
/media/FAA_Aerospace_Forecasts_FY_2018-2038.pdf.

6. The quotation is from the DART website about the Inwood/Love Field
Station.

7. Benjamin Schneider, "CityLab University: Induced Demand," *CityLab*,
September 6, 2018, https://www.citylab.com/transportation/2018/09
/citylab-university-induced-demand/569455/.

8. Jan Gehl, conversation with author, June 27, 2013.

Chapter 7: Inequities Built into Megaregions

1. For a more complete discussion of these urban growth patterns, see

"How the Metropolis Split Apart," chapter 5 in *The Fractured Metropolis: Improving the New City, Restoring the Old City, Reshaping the Region,* by the author (New York: HarperCollins, 1995). The book is available in a reprint edition by Westview Press and on Kindle through Routledge, 2018.

2. Alana Semuels, "The Epicenter of American Inequality," *Atlantic,* September 23, 2016.

3. Kenneth Jackson, *Crabgrass Frontier: The Suburbanization of the United States* (New York and Oxford: Oxford University Press, 1985). See, in particular, chapter 11: "Federal Subsidy and the Suburban Dream: How Washington Changed the American House Market." See also "The Roads Not Taken: How Government Policies Promote Economic Segregation and Suburban Sprawl," chapter 4 in *Place Matters: Metropolitics for the Twenty-First Century* (3rd edition), by Peter Dreier, John Mollenkopf, and Todd Swanstrom (Lawrence, KS: University Press of Kansas, 2014).

4. "Understanding Fair Housing," *Clearinghouse Publication 42,* US Commission on Civil Rights (February 1973).

5. Jackson, *Crabgrass Frontier,* 216–218.

6. Richard Rothstein, *The Color of Law: A Forgotten History of How Our Government Segregated America* (New York and London: Liveright Publication Corp., 2018).

7. William Julius Wilson, *The Truly Disadvantaged: The Inner City, the Underclass, and Public Policy* (Chicago: University of Chicago Press, 2012).

8. Dreier, Mollenkopf, and Swanstrom, *Place Matters,* 59–102.

9. Ruth Glass, *London: Aspects of Change* (London: MacGibbon and Kee, 1964), xvii.

10. Matthew Desmond, *Evicted: Poverty and Profit in the American City* (New York: Crown, 2016).

11. A good account of the contrast between relatively small gentrifying areas and the continued decline of older inner-city neighborhoods is *The Divided City: Poverty and Prosperity in Urban America* by Alan Mallach (Washington, DC: Island Press, 2018).

12. "Median Sales Price of Houses Sold," Federal Reserve Bank of St. Louis Economic Data, https://fred.stlouisfed.org/series/MSPUS.

13. Jill P. Capuzzo, "Harding Township, N.J.: A Historic Place That Feels Like the Country," *New York Times*, March 31, 2019.

14. See the discussion of exclusionary zoning in *Reinventing Development Regulations* by the author and Brian W. Blaesser (Cambridge, MA: Lincoln Institute of Land Policy, 2017), 125–128.

Chapter 8: Reducing Inequality in Megaregions

1. *Fourth Regional Plan for the New York–New Jersey–Connecticut Metropolitan Area*, Regional Plan Association, 2017, 22–25.

2. The Google maps for this location show no tenants for many of the stores, and the closed and vacant Kmart is visible in Google Street View. Note also the small number of cars in the parking lots.

3. The regulations for the Inclusionary Housing Program are found in Sections 23-154 and 23-90 of the NYC Zoning Resolution, and maps of designated areas are in Appendix F of the Zoning Resolution.

4. Published in January 2018.

5. See the discussion of accessory dwelling units on existing house lots in *Reinventing Development Regulations* by the author and Brian W. Blaesser (Cambridge, MA: Lincoln Institute of Land Policy, 2017), 132–137.

6. Allowing a mixture of lot sizes while preserving overall density requirements is also discussed in Barnett and Blaesser, *Reinventing Development Regulations*, 137.

Chapter 9: Adapting Governmental Structures to Manage Megaregions

1. J. W. Powell, *Report on the Lands of the Arid Region of the United States*, US Department of the Interior, 1878. A facsimile of the 1879 edition, with a new introduction by T. H. Watkins, was published by the Harvard Common Press in 1983, and other reprints are also available.

2. Article 1, Section 10, Clause 3 of the US Constitution: "No State shall, without the Consent of Congress, . . . enter into any Agreement or Compact with another State . . ."

3. Arizona initially withheld its signature.

4. See the notice by the National Oceanic and Atmospheric Administration (which administers the provisions of the Coastal Zone Management Act) of July 7, 2011, as published in the *Federal Register*.

5. Myron Orfield, a law professor at the University of Minnesota, wrote an

influential book titled *Metropolitics* (Washington, DC: Brookings Institution Press, 1997), which described how the Metropolitan Council came to be and how it works, bringing to this book his experience as a state legislator. Orfield advocated the Twin Cities Metropolitan Council as a template for regional government. Orfield is also the coauthor of a later book, *Region: Planning the Future of the Twin Cities* (Minneapolis: University of Minnesota Press, 2010), which investigates solutions to the many regional problems that the Metropolitan Council has been unable to solve, especially school segregation and unequal education funding.

Chapter 10: Rewriting Local Regulations to Promote Sustainability and Equity

1. Points made in this chapter are discussed in much greater detail in *Reinventing Development Regulations* by the author and Brian W. Blaesser (Cambridge, MA: Lincoln Institute of Land Policy, 2017).

2. Barnett and Blaesser, *Reinventing Development Regulations*, 49–54.

3. Barnett and Blaesser, 54–62.

Index

About the Author

Jonathan Barnett is one of the pioneers of the modern practice of city design, a discipline firmly grounded in current political, social, and economic realities. He was the director of urban design for the New York City Planning Department in the administration of Mayor John Lindsay. His book about innovations created in New York, *Urban Design as Public Policy*, was a strong influence in establishing urban design as a necessary element of local government and in making urban design a well-recognized profession. His practice as a city-designer includes long-term consulting relationships with the cities of Charleston, Cleveland, Kansas City, Nashville, Norfolk, Miami, Omaha, and Pittsburgh, and with the cities of Tianjin and Xiamen in China. He has also been the urban design advisor for several large-scale projects in Korea.

Jonathan has written many other books, book chapters, and articles about urban design. His most recent book, written with real estate lawyer Brian W. Blaesser, is *Reinventing Development Regulations*, which shows how to use government controls to implement urban design and sustainability concepts. Another recent book for Island Press, written with Larry Beasley, the former planning director for Vancouver, Canada, is *Ecodesign for Cities and Suburbs.* It demon-strates proven ways of integrating city design and environmental sus-tainability, drawing on many examples from around the world.

Jonathan is a Fellow of the Penn Institute for Urban Research and a professor emeritus of City and Regional Planning at the University of Pennsylvania. A graduate of Yale and the University of Cambridge, he is also a Fellow of the American Institute of Architects and of the American Institute of Certified Planners.